D1204118

DEALING
WITH THING
THIS
CALLED LIFE

The Self-Help Book for ALL Ages

CHRIS SUMLIN

Book Design & Production
Columbus Publishing Lab
www.ColumbusPublishingLab.com

Copyright © 2016 by Chris Sumlin
LCCN 2016936310

All rights reserved. This book, or parts thereof, may not be
reproduced in any form without permission.

Papaerback ISBN 978-1-63337-099-9
E-book ISBN 978-1-63337-100-2

Printed in the United States of America
1 3 5 7 9 10 8 6 4 2

"Greatness is not this wonderful, esoteric, elusive, God-like feature that only the special among us will ever taste, it's something that truly exists in all of us."

– Will Smith

To my beautiful mother, Monica, who has been the perfect personification of love and light in my life. She has lifted me in love more times than I can count. I have been able to do so much because of her endless love and support. My heart's utterance is to make her proud not just of the work that I do, but for the man that I am. Thank you, Mom.

To my father, ET, who was the perfect role model growing up. He was the first example I saw of true faith, hard work and manhood. His countless life lessons are ones that will stick with me forever. This book is an ode to him as he inspired many of the lessons in this book. Thank you, Dad!

To my family, friends, and loved ones. Thank you for loving me simply for who I am. For your prayers, well wishes and positive energy. Without you all, there would be no, THE Chris Sumlin. Thank you.

INTRODUCTION

LIFE CAN BE SOMETHING TO DEAL WITH; life has its good, its bad, times that are happy and sad. One thing I love to do to deal with life is read self-help books. Nothing makes me happier than being in a quiet space, with a book in-hand. I have read some fantastic books too. Some of my favorites include, *What I Know for Sure* by Oprah Winfrey, *How to Win at the Sport of Business* by Mark Cuban and my all time favorite, *The Four Agreements* by Don Miguel Ruiz. I do my best to buy my books, read them and pass them along to friends. Unfortunately, more times than not my friends don't read the books I recommend. "They're too long," they say. "That book is too deep," they express. Or my absolute favorite, "I hate reading it's boring." This bothered me because I know how important reading is and how impactful reading can be. So I asked myself, "What can I do to get more people like me: who are young, ambitious and busy, to actually sit down and read a book?" I thought maybe it was the books I was reading, and maybe I should find more books that were about self-help and written by young adults. I went to the library in hopes of finding a book that had the inspiration of Oprah Winfrey with the relatability of someone like a college student—a book that was as entertaining and comical just as much as it was inspiring and insightful. To my surprise, I could not find any. I researched young authors, black authors, books "for young adults" and through my search, I found nothing that really spoke to me. I knew that if I could not find books that spoke to me there was no way I could find books that spoke to my peers.

Then the famous Gandhi quote came to me, "Be the change you wish you see," and I was then inspired to write my own self-help book. My intention with this book is to speak to my generation and share my story. I know I do not have all the answers, but I know I can craft my words in a way that will inspire and uplift my millennial peers. After reading countless journal entries of mine, Facebook statuses, tweets and seeing old Instagram posts, I have come up with twelve life lessons that I have learned. I pray that after reading this book you are inspired, moved and as excited about your future as I am about mine.

As you read and learn about my story, enjoy it for what it is—life, my life, told from my eyes. If nothing else, I am sure you'll be entertained and will tell your friends of my adventures. This book discusses friendships, self-esteem and making the best of life. I am no better than anyone else, just another ambitious person who decided to write their story. You and I are no different; I encourage you to do the same and share your story. It is safe to say that we all have lives that are blessed with laughs, hugs, tears and experiences. Share these things; you never know what your story will do for someone else. We all want happiness, the freedom to express ourselves freely and reassurance that the future is promising, and I just hope this book provides some of that for you.

I AM SEEDS

OUR WORDS ARE POWERFUL and hold weight. Our words have the power to heal, to harm, to hurt or cure. Of all of the many words in our world, I believe that "I AM" are two of the more potent. Day in and day out we consistently use I AMs to describe how we are feeling. We may say:

I AM bored.

I AM tired.

Or I AM broke.

Little do many of us know the effect, magic and weight that these two words carry. "I AMs" are so important because "I AMs" are what you call yourself. No one else can give you an "I AM." When you use these words, they are a pure and personal expression of how you are in that present moment. Not only are "I AMs" personal feelings, but they are also seeds that feed and create your world.

Imagine your life as a magical garden, and in your garden, there is a soil. This soil has the power to grow any kind of seed you put into it. If you put seeds of faith in your soil, faith grows; if you put seeds of doubt, doubt grows. You are the creator of this garden by the words you speak. That is how life is.

There is a bigger force working endlessly responding to our words. Some call it The Universe. The Power, I call it God. Whatever you call it, it is listening and working with you to create your garden. Now that we know this, we are going to use our "I AM" seeds intentionally. We are going to delete the bad "I AM seeds" and plant new ones.

In this book each chapter is equipped with a powerful "I AM" good seed that you can use for your life's garden. Use them and use them often. Remember, every time you say an "I AM" statement you are planting and nourishing that seed in your garden. With this book, you get twelve, but I encourage you to create positive I AMs daily and watch your garden flourish. As with any planting results may not be instantaneous, but keep the faith and do not give up. We have the power to change our lives, so let's rise to the challenge and make it happen. We deserve it!

1

STINKIN' THINKIN'

DO YOU HAVE PEOPLE IN YOUR LIFE who are always smiling? People who seem to be resilient and never let things get them down? These kinds of folks find the good in every situation and always have a positive attitude. If you do, great. Keep these kinds of people around you because they are rare. Most of the people I encounter are so "realistic" they are not optimistic. When I was a young boy that was 80 percent of the people I saw growing up. To this day, I still don't have many people in my life who are the "happy-go-lucky" type, and boy does that suck. I must say, though, if there was one person I saw growing up who embodied these features, it would be my dad.

Growing up my dad was the most optimistic, positive and happy person I knew. No matter what came his way my dad always had a smile on his face. People often talk about my big Kool-Aid smile, but it's only a diluted replica of the smile I saw on my dad's face as a kid. My dad's smile would stretch from ear-to-ear and it had the ability to light up an entire room. The happiness my dad displayed wasn't just in his smile, it was in his spirit. It was who he was. Being around my dad was always a good time because he always did what he could to crack jokes and inspire people. I believe that my dad's innate positive attitude is what led him to become a preacher.

My dad was a pastor and preacher from the time he was nineteen years old. All of my young adult years consisted of church, church and more church. Every Sunday my family was the first one to the church and the last one to leave the church. Our church was small, but Dad used to preach like there were a million people there. He was very easy to listen to and a great speaker. My dad had a way of weaving comedy and inspiration into his sermons in a way that was very relatable and impactful.

I don't remember all of his sermons of course, but there was one I remember, "Dare to Dream." I had to have been about thirteen years old around the time of this sermon. Nonetheless, this sermon had elements in its teachings that still resonate with me to this day.

"Dare to Dream" was a good sermon; it was about believing in yourself enough to dream. When preaching this sermon, my dad used biblical references to support his topic and some life stories to conceptualize his big ideas. These ideas were:

Have faith.

Keep a positive perspective.

Dream big.

When my dad was up there preaching everyone seemed to be moved and touched by his words. Church members were jumping up and down, screaming and shouting. I could tell that my dad was bringing hope to people.

I was shy in church back then, so I was quiet and unfazed by everything around me. As I sat there in my church clothes, head down with my Nintendo DS in-hand, I heard a sentence that hit my core.

"Never have stinkin' thinkin.'" Those were the words my dad said that I will never forget.

When he made that statement, I immediately dropped my Nintendo DS to hear what it was my dad was saying. He went on and on about having a positive mindset and perspective.

I knew that this was the secret to my dad's smile and positive attitude—the idea of never having stinkin' thinkin'.

He went on and on and said statements like:

"Always see the good in every situation."

"Always see the best in yourself."

"Always look for the good in everyone you meet."

After I left the church that Sunday, I made the decision that I was going to move forward without stinkin' thinkin'. In retrospect, I think that this decision was a little ambitious for someone of my age. I was so young, but I knew for sure that I was going to see the best in every situation from that moment on and be super optimistic. It wasn't long before my idea of not having stinkin' thinkin' was put to the test when it came time for me to start high school.

Starting high school was one of the biggest moments in my life.

Growing up in Columbus, I went to charter schools from kindergarten until the sixth grade. In the seventh and eighth grade, I went to smaller, newer charter schools. When I graduated from the eighth grade, I was so nervous about what was to happen next because I did not know which school I wanted to attend. I knew I had to find a school that was close to home and one that would provide me with the best education possible. During that summer, my parents and I searched religiously for a suitable high school for me. I searched tirelessly for the right school until one day my search came to an end.

One day, my friend Ellen told me about the high school she planned to attend. Ellen was brilliant, always on the top of her game, and I knew that if she was going to any school, then that school had to be a good one. The school Ellen decided to attend was called The Charles School at Ohio Dominican University. The school was in its second year of existence and very new. I was fascinated by The Charles School. I learned early on that when I completed my high school education, I would be in the second graduating class in the school's history. The school was family orientated, and every staff member was young and energetic. After attending orientations and talking to the staff, the school resonated with my heart, and I knew that The Charles School was the school for me.

After I had been accepted, I told everyone I could about my new-found school. I was an ambassador for my high school before classes even began. After much anticipation, it was time for the first day of class. On that first day of school, all of my excitement went away when I walked into the cafeteria for the first time. I found myself experiencing the "stinkin' thinkin'" my dad preached about. Walking into the cafeteria was a lot for me. Everyone had on their first-day-of-school outfits. Everyone seemed so ready with their fresh sneakers and all their school supplies. On the other hand, I was terrified. I think my fear came from the fact that I didn't have the best middle school experience. In middle school I was tormented by my peers and the cafeteria was where a lot of my bullying happened. I used to get "riffed down" (as it was called) for everything about myself: the way I walked, talked and dressed. My worst fear was going through that again in high school. My stinkin' thinkin' got the best of me, and I decided that I would not get bullied in high school.

I decided I would be silent and stay out of everyone's way. I figured if I played it cool and never talked I would be okay and reduce the risk of being bullied. So with my stinkin' thinkin', I decided to be invisible, remain quiet and fade into the background. Surprisingly, my plan worked. The first day of school was a breeze. I was silent and invisible, and no one ever bothered me. My stinkin' thinkin' was strong, but I still had an innate urge to be outgoing and social. It was not until I met a friend named Zach that I finally got over my stinkin' thinkin' and decided to be myself.

I will never forget the conversation that changed the trajectory of my high school journey; it happened right after lunch period. Lunch has always been my favorite part of the day. When I got to the cafeteria for lunch on the first day of school, I knew my day was going to get better. As I sat in the cafeteria eating fruit and drinking orange juice, I saw a guy named Zach. Zach was the coolest. I recall admiring his style because Zach had on name-brand clothes from head to toe. Zach's outfit was way better than mine, and he carried himself with confidence that commanded respect from our peers.

After lunch, I had a class with Zach. We sat next to each other at the same table in the computer lab. He was cool, humble and talked to everyone. Although I could tell he was a nice person, I could not stop staring at his watch. The watch Zach wore was beige, bulky and had lots of buttons on it. I didn't like it at all. I knew I had stinkin' thinkin' towards the watch, but I didn't care because I simply thought it was ugly.

The watch captivated my attention so much that I had to ask Zach where he got it from and why he wore it. So I asked Zach, "Hey, man. What kind of watch is that? It's nice."

I knew the watch didn't look nice, but I decided not to begin our conversation with an insult, so I said something nice to start a positive dialogue.

I imagined Zach saying the watch was a gift from a younger sibling or that it was something he wore out of convenience. I couldn't conceive that he liked the watch. Zach laughed and said, "It's a CASIO G-Shock watch. I had wanted this one for quite some time now, but they are very expensive. I had to wait a couple of months to get this one."

The look on my face was one you had to see. I was floored by his response because I expected to hear something entirely different. My mind was completely blown. However, I couldn't let the conversation end there, so I decided to let my deep interest take over. I asked, "Well, why are they so expensive? How much do they cost?"

Zach smiled and humbly informed me, "G-Shocks are indestructible. These kinds of watches can withstand water, and you can drop them as many times as you'd like and they still don't break."

"Wow? How much do they run for?" I asked.

"Well, you can get a cheap one from a superstore for about fifty dollars, but if you want one like this, it will run you about one hundred and fifty dollars," Zach said.

After Zach had told me all the specifics and perks of having a G-Shock watch, he showed me a promotional video online. In the video, I saw a sledgehammer tested on the watch. Zach was right; the watch was indestructible and therefore, very cool. As others heard our conversation, people started expressing how they had heard of the watches and how much they yearned to have a G-Shock.

Following that interaction, I was cured of my stinkin' thinkin'. I thought if maybe I was wrong about the watch then maybe I was wrong about myself too. When judging Zach's watch, I completely disregarded everything good about it and labeled it as ugly. In my social interactions, I did the same thing. I never considered how nice, funny or great I was. I was so wrapped up in my stinkin' thinkin' that I lost who I truly was.

The lesson to learn from this experience is never to have stinkin' thinkin'. Always remember that you are great! I promise! We all have greatness inside of us; sometimes we just don't take the time to see it within ourselves. Next time you feel insecure or are being a little hard on yourself just say, "Everything is fine. I will not let this stinkin' thinkin' get the best of me." Having that attitude will change the trajectory of your self-esteem, and you will begin to view situations differently. I know I do.

The tape that we continually play in our minds has to be a good one. We have to water our minds with positive thoughts, and an ample amount of support and love. You would never plant a seed in the ground with the intention to tear it down or let it nurture itself. Our minds are the same way. Make a mandate to treasure your life and mind. Always keep your thoughts on your best. Always remind yourself that you are awesome simply because there is only one you. You are the only you that we have in this world. That sense of value is one that should ruminate in your mind daily.

Years later after that conversation with Zach I ordered the same watch he had. I was eighteen years old when I could finally afford one. It was one of the best watches I ever had. Thanks for the tip, Zach!

I AM SEED:

I am not a possessor of stinkin' thinkin'.

2

SUN IN THE STORM

ONE THING I KNOW ABOUT DEALING WITH LIFE is that perspective is everything. Life is complex and it's not easy. If there is one thing we can all relate to it's hard times. A way to combat and stay active in these hard times is to keep a positive perspective. A significant moment that taught me this lesson of a positive outlook is when I lived with my grandparents.

My family has always been very tight. As far back as I can remember I recall always having magical family memories during Halloween, Thanksgiving, and Christmas seasons. It was nothing for our family to come together for a cookout, birthday or a family night. There's a nice group of us too. Between my mother, my aunt, and my uncle, my grandparents have twelve grandchildren ranging from ages twelve to twenty-three. In retrospect, I do not know how my grandparents put up with all of us. We are all so close in age and used to be so in love with each other's company.

Every chance we could get we would all spend the night at our grandparents', all twelve of us. My grandparents would have a house full of us cousins, and we loved it. There would be times when we would stay up until two and three in the morning listening to music, eating Twizzlers and playing video games. It's funny because when we would all have sleepovers I was always picked on for being the one who would go to sleep first. Nights were long, and we would have so much fun; those sleepover memories are ones that will stick with me forever.

Unfortunately, when everyone got older we began to have girlfriends, boyfriends, other friends, and each of us followed our own path. We are not as close as we once were, but even today we reminisce on the phenomenal sleepovers we would have at our Nanny and Papa's house.

Nanny and Papa's house was the hangout spot. I'll never forget hanging with my cousin Jonathan. Jonathan was the first person I looked up to because he always had the gift to convince everyone around him to do what he wanted them to do. One time when I was six years old, Jonathan had assured my mother, his mother and my grandmother enough to allow us to play *Mortal Kombat*. Times were different back then; a person couldn't turn on the television and see all the things on TV that we do now. Back then we would watch *Barney*, *Arthur*, and *Rugrats*. *Mortal Kombat* was a very bloody, gory game that was a little mature for us young guys at that time. Jonathan felt otherwise. He convinced all the adults in the house that it was okay and that we should play *Mortal Kombat*. I remember us playing that game for hours at Nanny and Papa's house that weekend night. I was getting the hang of the game, and before I knew it, it was time to head home.

"Sumlin kids let's go," my mother yelled up the stairs to where we were playing.

As a young guy, I was so distraught. I wanted to play longer. Jonathan and I finished our round of the game, and he and I went downstairs. As I walked down the stairs, my face was puffy red because I wanted to stay and play longer. I hugged my grandparents and headed out to the car. During the drive home, I put my head down and began to cry.

Jonathan had a bedroom at Nanny and Papa's house, and I was so jealous that he lived with them. I always dreamed of living with my nanny and papa, so I could be with them and play video games. My grandparents have always been my favorite people for as long as I can remember. I love my grandparents so much, and I was infatuated with their house. As I got older, I began to drift away from the fantasy of living with my grandparents. Oddly enough when I was sixteen I got exactly what I had once hoped for.

When I was sixteen, I had to move in with my grandparents. This transition was due to a lot of drama and turmoil at my house. I will never forget the heated arguments that transpired during this time in my life. It was a dark time for my family, and me. Every day was a soap opera; something was always going down. Walking home from school I recall always being nervous just envisioning what the story would be for that day. I would ask myself: Who betrayed my father? Who offended my mom? Who disrespected our home? Drama and turmoil became the norm for our household during this time in my life.

One night there was a major fight at my house. I can't recollect exactly what happened because I was asleep, but I remember my mother waking my siblings and me up, instructing us to pack our belongings because we were leaving for the night. This night was the first time I remember ever having to leave my room so abruptly. Although there was a lot of turmoil in our home, it was comfortable. I loved the house we lived in. The house was big consisting of three levels, with three living rooms, and six bedrooms. We all had our own space. I did not want to leave my house for any period longer than I had to. But that night we left and moved to my grandparents' house for a period of time.

Switching over to live with my grandparents was uncomfortable for everyone. My grandparents lived alone in a nice two-bedroom home. It was perfect and fitting for them. It was not the kind of living space for five more people to come live, but like good family, my grandparents opened their doors for me, my three siblings and my mom. We lived with my grandparents for about a month before returning to our big home. The first few nights were hard. I remember having to share a pallet on the floor with my brother and having only one central television. Initially I was very pessimistic, thinking only about how much I was missing out on. Like most teenagers I wanted my own space and stupid things like my own TV. My mother was stressed as her life took a major turn. I can't reiterate how uncomfortable things were physically, emotionally and spiritually, but everything just felt very different. My grandparents were very sensitive to the fact that things were not the best.

My papa was very adamant about trying to do his best to make us happy because he knew we weren't happy. He knew my siblings wanted our space and to be, well, teenagers. Nevertheless, Papa kept us all laughing with his joyous spirit and jokes. At the time, Papa was battling colon cancer, but you'd never know that because he was so strong and full of energy. Papa stood tall as he was well over six feet; he was frail but had a personality that could fill any room. I always admired my papa. He was a great man and made me smile whenever we would talk. During this time of living with him, the peak of my day was leaving school and heading to my grandparents' home. I would walk in, jump on Papa's bed and talk to him for hours telling him about my day. He was always so eager to listen and fascinated with every word that I said. Papa and I got very close during this hectic time in my life. We also did a lot of praying. We prayed every morning before my siblings and I would head out to school. I still remember some of those prayers we would pray in the mornings. Papa was very humorous, but one thing he did not play about was his prayer. I know for sure that my life would not have panned out in some aspects as it did had it not been for Papa praying for me. Papa was the man. He was truly the sunshine in the midst of the storm.

A couple of weeks after staying with my grandparents things settled down at my home. My mother, siblings and I moved back home with my father. Unfortunately, just a few short months later Papa died from his battle with cancer. It was a severe blow to my family and happened very suddenly. Papa never got to see me graduate from high school, get accepted into Morehouse or hear of me meeting any of these stars. Papa would have loved to hear how I met Rihanna. But he isn't here. I always say, had it not been for my family going through our struggle, I may have never gotten as close to Papa as I did during that time. The family drama is what led to us moving in with him and my grandmother. I am grateful for that rough time. I am grateful for living in their small home. I am grateful for the drama within my family at that point. All of that allowed me to get closer to my grandfather before he passed.

We all have heartaches; we all have painful experiences or times where we do not know what to do. But with that, I promise there is always a sun still up there during a thunderstorm. It may be hard to find, or locate, but I promise you it is there. The sun doesn't go away forever just because there is a bad storm. If you go up high enough, you can always find it. It is just like when you are flying on an airplane. My favorite part of flying is when you get past the clouds and the storm, and there you see the beautiful sun radiating down on the clouds.

Life never gets too cold on us. There is always something to be grateful for; that's your sun in the storm. Pregnant mothers, I am sure pregnancy is terrible, but just imagine what a joy it is going to be when that young child is in your arms. Young college students, I know midterms and finals can be hard, but you are at the peak of your physical life. Everyone loves their young college days; work hard and study but always be grateful that you are in school. Everyone has something they can be grateful for and acknowledge.

When I am having a bad day, and I feel like my life is under a storm, I get still and breathe. I simply thank God for my breath, that there is a warm heart beating in the center of my chest. I think to myself, wow, things may not be perfect, but I am still here. Still alive and well. Gratitude is so powerful. Always remember to appreciate the small things that may be passing you by. Don't get so caught up in your struggle or discomfort that you miss something beautiful that you may lose later. There is always a sun during every storm; having this perspective makes dealing with life a tad bit easier.

Thanks, Papa. I know you will never get to read this book, but you taught me a valuable lesson. You were truly the personification of the sunshine in the midst of the storm. Your spirit and life experiences continue to impact me to this very day. Thank you!

I AM SEED:

I am grateful there is always sun to get me through a storm.

3

FEED YOUR FAITH, STARVE YOUR FEAR

FEAR IS ONE OF THE MOST POWERFUL WEAPONS life throws our way that can make dealing with life rather difficult. Fear is strong—it is crippling and has the power to stop us from reaching our dreams. I once had a conversation with my father about fear. He told me that fear can be defined as False Evidence Appearing to be Real. Often the idea of what we are afraid of is not a real thing, but merely only a product of our imagination and ignorance.

Think about that. Think of the last time you were afraid of something. I am sure that you were probably fearful because you were ignorant of some aspect of your situation. To cope with your ignorance of the situation, you draft some false, dramatic scenario in your mind and convince yourself that it is your destiny.

When I first started flying to and from school instead of taking the bus across the country, I was always very fearful that I would die. Every time I would get on a plane I was never 100 percent certain that I would land safely. Because of this uncertainty, I would imagine these dramatic scenarios where I would be on a plane and a pipe would burst or the pilot would get sick and accidentally crash the plane. I had no evidence that any of that could happen, but I was not certain that I was going to land safely. On a flight to Texas, I once shared my plane crash imaginations with a woman I was sitting next to. The woman was older and well dressed. She and I were sitting next to her husband. I could tell that the two of them had flown a lot. Unfortunately, I was screaming and calling on Jesus every bump and gesture during our flight. As I sat there very stiffly, eyes closed and fearful, the woman tapped me on the shoulder and said, "You don't fly often do you?"

"No," I replied. That flight to Texas was the third flight of my life.

"Just relax and have faith in the pilot and crafters of the plane." She said this to me in such a compassionate tone.

As we conversed, we hit another bump of turbulence, and I still jerked and was scared. After collecting myself, I said to her, "How can you remain so calm and not be afraid?"

"Because I have more faith in the pilot than fear of crashing."

This flight was a major learning experience for me. After this conversation, I had an epiphany about fear and how to deal with it in my life. From that flight I learned when dealing with fear in our lives it is not so much about convincing ourselves that fear, in essence, doesn't exist, but acknowledging the fear and combatting it with faith. It is imperative that when dealing with fear we starve it and feed our faith. Following that flight, this was the first time I was able to articulate this idea to myself in this way. To my surprise I had practiced this idea when I was seventeen and working at Taco Bell.

Taco Bell was just one of the many jobs I held during my teenage years. The first internship I ever had was a marketing internship at a private college in Ohio. I got that job fresh out of my sophomore year of high school. Working was fun for me, and once I started working I never wanted to stop. I got gratification from work knowing that I was earning money for myself in an honest way. The internship I worked was great, but ended after eight weeks. I always knew that it was going to end, so during the seventh week of my internship I picked up another job. This was when I landed my second job at the great Taco Bell.

Contrary to a lot of my school mates who worked, I was proud to work at a fast food restaurant. One of the reasons I loved working at Taco Bell so much was because it had a uniform. Having a uniform to go to work in gave me this sense of purpose. I felt like Superman. Every day I would catch the bus and I would be so proud to have on my Taco Bell hat and polo. When talking to customers at my job, they would know my name without me having to introduce myself because they would read my name tag. Taco Bell made me feel so cool.

Although I have always been a go-getter and self-sufficient, I didn't snag this job on my own. I got the job after a recommendation from my brother Orlando who was already a rock star at the restaurant I applied to. Orlando had been the top service champion for a few short months at

Taco Bell, and he was deeply appreciated. He would go in for hours and hours in a week, taking shifts, getting productivity up and doing his job so perfectly. When the managers at his location heard that he had a brother and that I wanted to work there, it was a sealed deal. I applied, went in for an interview and was hired on the spot. In May of 2011, I started my Taco Bell journey.

Orlando and I made quite a splash at Taco Bell. Of course, he and I looked alike, we had the same uniform and same facial features. The comparisons to Orlando were endless. Everything I did had to be as good as Orlando. I had to have as much personality, take orders as fast, and have as much knowledge of product as he did. My first few days of going to work I would be so happy and excited to be there. But shortly all of that excitement and positive energy would fade away because I simply couldn't keep up with Orlando. He set the bar high. In retrospect it was funny because of how insecure I was about everything. I was seen and not heard, keeping to myself and counting down the minutes when I could finally go home. I did not enjoy days at Taco Bell, but if there was one day of the week I enjoyed least it was Thursday.

For some reason Thursday shifts at Taco Bell were always the busiest. I don't know what it was about Thursdays that made everyone crave burritos and tacos so much, but they did. On Thursdays I would usually insist on staying in the back, doing the dishes and hiding where I couldn't be seen or heard. I knew Orlando would be the superstar doing his thing, and he was. Orlando would be in the front of the store at the drive-thru window being a beast. On Thursdays, the line of cars would always wrap around our parking lot as customers were eagerly waiting to be served. Somehow my brother always had a way of getting a car out of the queue in less than seventy-five seconds. Every so often Orlando would catch a two-second break, and he would come back to me, at the dishwasher. He would be all revved up from all of the work that was happening at the front. I, on the other hand, would be in the back of the store sad and soaked from the dishwater as I washed dishes as fast as I could. Orlando would always look at me and say, "If you stay back here and do dishes all the time that is all you will do."

He stated that all the time. For me, I enjoyed doing the dishes because I knew I was safe and no one would bother me. I didn't have to deal with any customers and I didn't have to worry about keeping anything under seconds; I was content. I was genuinely afraid of the drive thru—it just seemed like there was a lot going on.

I always imagined myself going too slow, angering customers and getting fired. Doing the dishes, singing Mariah Carey and keeping to myself was enough for me. Oddly enough, that Thursday my world was turned upside down.

That Thursday night our manager came back to the dish pit in a frenzy and said, "Chris, you will be backing up your brother on drive thru tonight for training. Don't let us down."

I only had a few hours left of my shift, but I was terrified. You should have seen the look on my face when my manager said those words to me. I remember trying to come up with any and every excuse I could think of as to why I shouldn't be on drive thru. Nothing worked. Orlando returned to where we were.

"Christopher, it's a Thursday night, and we are hitting dinner hours. You better bring it, but we will make it fun."

I had no words; I gave him one of my epic fake smiles. I knew that it was about to go down. As I put on my headset, I imagined every worst thing that could happen on drive thru. I thought someone would curse me out, throw a drink on me, and I would ruin the entire shift's flow. I was paralyzed with fear.

"You ready?" Orlando asked.

I walked right over to the window and the next thing you know I was working the drive thru. In the beginning, I was shaking with fear as I stood across from my brother. Orlando dealt with the customers through the headsets and took orders; it was my job to make the beverages and distribute the food to the customers. Initially I was a little awkward, but it was not bad at all. I began to have faith in my people skills and my ability always to smile. I have always had an innate ability to be social and good with people. In this instance, I utilized that skill the best I could. I simply did my best to smile and put as much personality into my job as I could.

An hour into the drive-thru experience everything seemed to be going well. The customers seemed very satisfied with our work. Throughout the shift customers kept making comments about how they loved that we were two brothers, working well together doing something with ourselves. The best thing ever was when our shift was coming to an end. In the last ten minutes of that shift our mom, dad and siblings rode through the drive thru and ordered. My mom always looked so proud. My dad would always do the most, asking for all types of extra steak and stuff. I would always put that additional cost right on the order too. Good times. My first day on the drive thru went well once I dispelled all those fearful thoughts about how I would bomb. It was a great start to my Taco Bell drive-thru journey.

About a month later Orlando went off to college to pursue his dream of music. It was just me there at Taco Bell to hold down the legacy and do my best. I did a pretty good job too, and because of his awesome training I became a beast on drive thru. Everyone on staff would always get so happy and excited when they knew I was the drive-thru attendant because I was so efficient. My manager once told me, "After all this time, I think you have finally gotten as good as your brother. If he comes back you may have to train him." Getting over my initial fear and having faith in myself worked out well. This was an excellent experience, and looking back I've learned a lot from it.

I hope through my story you learn to feed your faith and starve your fear. Don't ever let fear stop you from growth. Would I have been happy doing the dishes forever in the back of the restaurant? Probably not. Every time I went home my boxers were soaked with all the soapy water that would get on me. I also didn't like how the dish soap would dry out my hands. My hands looked like they belonged to a seventy-year-old gardener at the end of my shift. But that would have been my life had I not stepped out, starved my fear and had faith that I could do a good job as a drive-thru attendant.

You will have times in your life when you will be presented with an opportunity that may be unfamiliar or scary. Whether you're giving a presentation on a business proposal you have, or asking a girl out on a date, no matter what happens never let fear hold you back. Fear is such a powerful tool used by negative forces in our lives to hold us back from becoming who we were born to be. Ask yourself, how many times have I let fear hold me back? How many people do you know who never decided to go off to college because they were afraid of the financial burden? How many family members do you have who are afraid to get on a flight, so they never get to experience the beauty this world has to offer? How many friends are scared to get on the dance floor and break free every time you all go out to a party? Fear can creep on so many levels of our lives. The only way to win the battle over fear is not to give it power. Don't feed into negative thoughts. Remember how when I was doing dishes and wasn't on drive thru, all I could imagine was how horrible of an experience working the drive thru could be? Never once did I think to myself that I could make someone smile with my personality, or that I would get to spend quality time with my brother before he left for college. All of that would have been missed had I become a slave to my fear.

In life, feed the possibilities life gives you with faith and starve your insecurities and fear. Release your inhibitions. Be fearless and try. If whatever you decide to try doesn't work out, at least you tried. You deserve the right of venturing out simply for the possibility of succeeding. So get up, get out there and let go of fear. I hope that through your fearlessness you achieve great things. Always remember to feed your faith and starve your fear.

Thank you so much, Orlando. You were an excellent role model for me at work, and if it weren't for you I probably wouldn't have gotten that job. Because I worked at Taco Bell, I learned so much about customer service, people, and resilience. I enjoyed our time at Taco Bell even if it was just for a month. It was one of the best months of the summer that year and for that I thank you.

I AM SEED:

I am feeding my faith and starving my fear.

4

GO THE EXTRA MILE

IF THERE IS ONE THING I KNOW FOR SURE when dealing with life, it is that sometimes the going gets tough. Sometimes we have to work hard and fight for the things we want. Growing up I always heard my parents say, "Anything worth having is worth fighting for." My parents worked so hard for everything they had and expected my siblings and me to do the same. This belief system taught me the importance of drive and work ethic. When I wanted a video game, I had to work for it. When I wanted the latest gadget or pair of sneakers, I had to work for it. Working hard to earn anything I wished for became the norm.

I can say with confidence that because of my childhood I thoroughly understand the concept of working hard for what you want. One thing I continue to struggle with is the ability to endure when "working hard" is still not enough. In life sometimes we try, and try, and try again and still do not get the results that we want. On some occasions we have to stretch ourselves to new limits, reach new heights and go the extra mile. My experience of getting accepted into Morehouse taught me this lesson more than I could have ever imagined.

Of all the things I have worked for, I must say that getting accepted into Morehouse College has truly been one of the highest achievements. By attending this great institution, I have been able to do things I would have never thought were imaginable. I have made amazing friends, learned so many new things and created awesome memories. Occasionally I reflect on my decisions and ponder that this journey through Morehouse could not have happened had I not worked for it and gone the extra mile.

Before Morehouse, I was just a regular kid in high school. My high school, The Charles School, is an early college high school that grants students the opportunity to attend college classes for free. The chance to attend college for free is great, but it comes at a great cost. The Charles School expects students to excel in their high school classes before even thinking about enrolling in college classes. I knew that I wanted to take college classes early, so I went the extra mile and through hard work I attended Ohio Dominican University at age sixteen. I enjoyed the early college experience. It was a great success knowing that I earned my spot in those classes.

After three years of being in The Charles School's early college program, I amassed sixty-two credit hours, earning myself an associate of arts degree at the age of nineteen.

During those three years, I worked hard and pushed myself. At Ohio Dominican, I read classic literature that I had never seen before, took social science classes that were rigorous, and English classes that challenged me to write more than I could ask.

Back when I received the news that I was on track to earn my associate of arts degree from Ohio Dominican, I knew that this was something to be proud of and acknowledge. I also knew that this degree was only the beginning of my intellectual journey. I felt that there was more I could do to make my family proud. My father dropped out of high school in the ninth grade to support his grandmother. My mother never received a bachelor's degree either. My mom and dad were married at the age of nineteen. I knew that because they got married young they never got to fulfill their dreams of going to college. As their child, I wanted to fulfill that dream.

During my last semester in The Charles School's early college program, I began searching for colleges where I could earn my bachelor's degree. That period of my life was a very stressful time. I had to take an ACT, research tons of schools, and make sure I was still on top of my current classes. All of this was very new to me and scary.

This process was scary because I had no idea what I was doing. I didn't know how much college costed, what city I wanted to go to college in, or how I would make it happen if I got accepted. After many Google searches, I applied to nine different colleges. The list was very random and sporadic. I heard certain teachers suggest that I apply to individual local schools like Baldwin Wallace and the University of Dayton. Others suggested that I continue my tenure at Ohio Dominican. One teacher named Shannon Taylor thought Morehouse was a good fit for me. At the time, I had never even heard of half these schools, including Morehouse, or seen their campuses. My family and I didn't have the money to travel around and do campus tours. I had no idea what I was getting myself into and what I would do next. Knowing this, I was nervous, but something in me just decided to step out of faith and apply to all these schools I had heard of hoping for the best.

While waiting for decision letters I took it upon myself to evaluate the schools more intimately. After researching schools like Baldwin Wallace, Pace University, Howard University and the other six schools I applied to, I was excited. I found out that all of the schools were great schools. Each institution had something I appreciated or valued. Interestingly enough, of all the schools on my list, for some reason, I could not get over Morehouse.

Morehouse became my obsession. When I watched videos online of Morehouse and saw how the students and alum spoke, something inside of me came alive. It felt right. Although I loved Morehouse for its branding of African American men, I knew that it would not be easy to get accepted. I knew that I would have to go the extra mile and give it my all if I were to get accepted and attend.

In December of 2012, I started to receive decision letters from my schools. I had gotten accepted into every college that had sent me a decision letter thus far. I was proud and felt accomplished, but I knew the acceptance letter that I wanted. On December 13, 2012 I got a letter from Morehouse. I was confident knowing that I sent them my resume with all my accolades, and just knew there was no way I could get denied. That evening I opened the letter with all this anticipation and anxiety. The letter was short and said that my application was deferred. Of course, being unfamiliar with the college admission process, the word deferred broke my heart. I thought I wasn't going to get accepted and that my life was over.

That night before I went to bed I prayed and cried that somehow the decision would be overturned. I remember laying on the floor of my bedroom crying my eyes out. Looking back on this moment it's quite comical to know that I laid on my bedroom floor crying in the dark for an hour, very dramatically, but it indeed happened.

After moments of laying there, my tears stopped, and I had an epiphany. I thought back to all the times I pushed myself beyond my limits to get what I wanted. I came to the conclusion that this situation was no different from my past. I told myself that if I wanted to get into Morehouse I would have to go the extra mile and show the admissions committee that I was worthy of acceptance.

The next day I went to school and discussed my frustration with an office associate named Mrs. Chelsea. Mrs. Chelsea worked at The Charles School and believed that I was destined for great things. She told me she would do everything in her power to help me get into this college. I told her my idea of writing Morehouse a letter and giving them a folder filled with reasons why I was worthy to attend this college. With the goal in mind, Mrs. Chelsea and I created a list of documents that discussed why I was fit for Morehouse. The materials presented community service work, I wrote a personal statement, Mrs. Chelsea wrote a letter of recommendation, and we even copied some honor certificates I had received from TCS. Together we went the extra mile. After we had sent everything off, I remember feeling relieved that it was going to work out. The wait seemed better this time around because I had gone the extra mile.

Following that moment, I went home every day from school expecting a letter to come in the mail with my acceptance. I began telling everyone I was going to Morehouse even though I had not been accepted yet. After much prayer and faith, on February 12, 2013 I got a massive package from Morehouse stating that I had been accepted into the college. It was a joyous experience. Everyone at my high school was so proud. Mrs. Chelsea was proud of me that it worked, Mrs. Shannon Taylor was proud of me, and most importantly I was proud of myself.

This entire experience taught me the importance of going the extra mile to get what you want. I think after knowing that I was going to receive my associates degree, I began to get cocky and comfortable. I forgot about how hard I had to work to get to where I was at that point. I was becoming comfortable just showing up and getting what I wanted. To get accepted to Morehouse, I knew I had to do more. Although I had applied, sent them my resume and did what I thought was "working hard," that was not enough. I had to turn up, push harder and go the extra mile.

In July of 2015 I posted an Instagram post that stated, "At 211 degrees, water is hot. At 212 degrees, it boils. And with boiling water comes steam and steam can power a locomotive. One extra degree…makes all the difference."

This principle is one that can also be applied to relationships and people. Going the extra mile can prove your loyalty or love to someone else. Think about mothers and how hard they try to go for their children when they want something. A mother will always find a way to make things happen for her children. Real parenthood is the best example of someone who continually goes the extra mile.

When you are stuck trying to achieve your dreams, ask yourself in any situation, "Am I going the extra mile to achieve my goal? Am I giving it all I've got?" You are brilliant, talented and awesome, but not everything you aspire to obtain will come easy. There's another great quote that says, "Life begins at the end of your comfort zone." If you are feeling uncomfortable now, know that the change taking place in your life is a beginning, not an ending.

I encourage you always to go the extra mile. Live your life at 212 degrees, always going after what you want. Whether it is through your studies, your career, or even your personal relationships, I promise you the reward is greater than your discomfort. I do not believe I would be where I am today or who I am today had it not been for the decision to go the extra mile. I don't think I would be a student at Morehouse.

Today, Mrs. Chelsea and I remain in touch. Mrs. Chelsea has had two babies and no longer works at my high school. Whenever I am in town, we catch up and do lunch. Every time I see her, I wear a Morehouse T-shirt, and we discuss my adventures at Morehouse. It's always a great time. Thanks, Mrs. Chelsea!

I AM SEED:

I am going the extra mile to achieve my dreams.

5

DO THE BEST YOU CAN

IF YOU ARE PERFECT, you will have read the previous chapters and instantly be able to apply these lessons to your life. You will know how to make meaningful friendships, accept criticism appropriately and be a master at dealing with this thing called life. For those of you who are perfect, congrats. You do not need to read this chapter because you know exactly what you are doing. For those of you like me who will read this book and feel good about it but still make mistakes, this chapter is for you.

I firmly believe that reading is excellent, and I recommend it often. I also believe in going to lectures, church and doing as much learning about life as we can through all of these self-help resources. I am sure all of these resources we are constantly bombarded with are good. I also firmly believe that the more self-help resources you utilize, the easier life will be. Unfortunately, after we read a book, go to a lecture or have an awesome spiritual experience, life is there waiting. Life is there waiting with its hardships, disappointments, and letdowns that test us in a plethora of ways. Sometimes we win, sometimes we learn, but the biggest key to success in dealing with life is applying the knowledge we learn and doing the best we can. If we operate our lives with the intention of being our best selves, that alone is enough. Always remember to try to do your best and I promise if you do that you will be okay.

I learned this lesson of doing my best the most my freshman year at Morehouse when I was part of the glee club. Being part of the glee club at Morehouse was a magical experience. The glee club has been around since 1911 and was founded on brotherhood, discipline and dedication. I had the honor of being part of the glee club for two years. In those two years, I learned so much. Day in and day out we would go to rehearsal. We would warm up for about fifteen to twenty minutes, our director would walk in, and rehearsal would officially begin. In that hour and a half I was in rehearsal, I was always expected to do my best. In the beginning, this was very hard for me.

When I first joined the glee club, I was timid. I came to college as a business major with no choral experience. While singing, I was surrounded by music majors and upperclassmen, and for them, singing was their passion. A lot of the guys in the glee club are very talented and can sing. In rehearsal, I would look at a lot of them and think, "Wow, it must be nice to know you can sing and sing with confidence."

I yearned for that confidence ever since my first day of being in the glee club. For the longest time I would sit in my section, fearful of criticism, and sing very quietly. I had no confidence in my singing abilities whatsoever, but nonetheless I would sit and just be happy to be part of the glee club.

One day I was tired of faking it and not giving it my all. I will never forget the day I finally conjured up enough courage to try and sing. I told myself that this would be the day I would put myself out there, sing with a full voice and go all out. At this time we hadn't rehearsed any chamber music, or anything too difficult; we were working on the National Anthem. I knew that I knew the words to the National Anthem, so I felt I was prepared to bring it. That entire day I was so excited for rehearsal. I went around all day, smiling from ear-to-ear excited for rehearsal. I knew I was going to prove to myself that I could do it.

After much anticipation, it was finally 4:00 p.m. and rehearsal was in session. The glee club at Morehouse has always been a very particular group. Our director takes his job very seriously and expects us all to do the same. Rehearsal is something serious, and this day was no different. That day in rehearsal we were emphasizing the importance of diction and enunciating every part of each word. When we worked on pronunciation we went very slowly, focusing on one word at a time for many trials until we got it right. It is an essential part of choral singing, but not the most fun. As we kept doing this, I began to lose my excitement, worried that we would run out of time and that I wouldn't get my moment.

After about fifteen more trials our director finally asked us to do the first verse all the way through. I was pumped; this was my chance, my time to go in. When our director raised his baton, I put my right index finger in my ear and belted out those first tenor notes as if I were Mariah Carey.

It was hilarious. You should have seen the look on my face and the effort in my heart. I could only imagine how foolish I looked. I thought I was killing it; no one could tell me otherwise. About ten seconds into the song, our director stopped the singing because something was wrong. At this moment I knew he was not concerned about me and my choral section, I mean how could he be? He had to have heard my full-out singing; I was sure it was good. As I was waiting for our director to instruct, I stood there proud, knowing I did well. To my surprise, our director looked over at my section and said, "First tenors, get on top of the pitch. You are missing it every time. And one of you, I do not know who it is, is in another octave flat. So it's in the wrong octave, and it's flat."

Again, it was the beginning of the year, so our director was patient. Some of the seniors, on the other hand, were less than pleased. I was so embarrassed. I knew it was me; I was the only one who was singing a tad bit higher than everyone in the section. Because my ear was untrained, I thought I was killing it, but, unfortunately, I wasn't doing anything but messing us up.

The rest of that rehearsal I pulled my finger out of my ear and made the effort to hear everyone around me so I could get better. Some of those brothers in the glee club were so talented, and so I would listen closely, mimic what they would do and try my best. From that moment on I continued to come out of my shell, believe in myself and do my best. My efforts must have meant something because later that semester I was one of a handful of freshmen selected to go on the Fall Tour.

Fall Tour is no joke; it is where only a select number of gentlemen in the chorus go to different cities and perform full concerts. In rehearsal, it's fun and supportive. We stop in the middle of songs to work on them, piece by piece. In a full-on concert, we arrive, we sing, and we keep going hoping for the best.

Fall Tour was a new experience for me and one that I sincerely enjoyed. One unique thing I remember about Fall Tour was that we performed a song in solfège. Solfège is a system for singing music notes where you sing using the solfège note names: do, re, mi, fa, sol, la and ti instead of the actual syllables and words. For me it was tricky because when singing, it is easy to memorize words, stories and ideas, but it is much harder trying to remember syllable notes that I had no connection to. I was terrified to sing in solfège on tour because I did not want to mess up. Going in I knew that this Fall Tour would be quite a challenge because of the solfège. And I was correct.

Our first stop on the Fall Tour was Charleston, North Carolina. The church there was so beautiful. It was grand, yet elegant and very traditional. Before our concert that evening, we did a sound check. The sound check is never really that long, it's just there for us to hear the acoustics of the place in which we are performing. During sound check, we rehearsed the solfège song we had learned in rehearsal. I was terrified and stumbled over my syllables profusely. It was atrocious. After we stopped, our director realized that some of us did not know what we were singing because we didn't take the necessary time to learn it on our own. I felt guilty because I knew I was in that category. Our director was not pleased. After he stated how disappointed in us he was, he then said, "If any of you get up here and do not know the song, I will stop the song during the performance and send whoever does not know it all the way home to Atlanta."

After he made that statement all I could do was imagine the reaction of the crowd when they saw me get kicked off the stage. I thought about how that conversation would go when I would call my mom and tell her what happened. I just knew I was going home. The sound check ended shortly after our director's "do better" speech.

After sound check, it was time for dinner. I could not even eat. As everyone else was calmly eating their food, I was panicking trying to figure out how I was going to learn the solfège song before the performance. I studied that sheet of music over and over until it was time to get dressed. As I got dressed for the concert, I said a small prayer asking God to help me get the words. After I had prayed I "let it go." I told myself I was going to do my best and that I was NOT going home.

As the concert began the crowd was giving us so much love; they seemed to really enjoy everything we sang. I felt a positive energy and it cheered me up. I knew it was going to be a good concert. After about seven songs we had an intermission, and the nerves came back. I asked one of my glee club brothers what the first song was that we were singing in Act Two. And sure enough, he told me it was the solfège song. Again I was so nervous. I quickly went to the side, prayed, and told myself again just to do my best and that I was not going to get sent home.

Shortly after that, we went back on stage. Our director announced that we were doing a song in solfège. My heart dropped. "Do the best you can, do the best you can" was the only thing running through my head.

Before I knew it, he was counting us in, and the song started. I took a deep breath, and before I could even gather what I was doing, I was up there singing in solfège and singing it correctly. I shocked myself at how well I did. Once the song was over and the crowd clapped, I wiped my forehead and released a big breath. I was sweating so hard, but after it was over I knew I had done well. The rest of the concert went well, and I sang on the entire Fall Tour that year and was not sent home. It was one of the most memorable experiences of my freshman year. I credit that whole experience to the fact that in that moment I did the best I could.

When dealing with life, it is always important to do the best we can. Sometimes we face challenges that we perceive as greater than our ability. When I joined the glee club, I often got nervous because I could not sing as well as my vocal counterparts. Sometimes I did not know the songs as well as others. All of those factors were not important. The important thing is that I did the best I could.

In this book, we will discuss pressing on, holding on, not letting fear hold us back and a plethora of other things. But in my opinion, this is the most important lesson of them all. Just do the best you can in everything that you do. Don't try and compare yourself to what the next person is doing. The same energy it takes to look to the right or left is wasted energy that you could have used in running your race. Always do your best to run your race. Each of our lives is equipped with its own set of life lessons, failures, and successes. In all of that, just make sure that you are always doing the best that you can. That is all you can do. When I was in the glee club was I the best singer? No. Did I know every single word, syllable, and pitch to perfection? No. But I always, no matter what, tried to do my best and I encourage you to do the same. If you move through life with the intention of being your absolute, truest, best self, that is all you can do. Sometimes you will win, sometimes you will lose, but you can never have regrets knowing you did the best you could.

That same year, I did so well after Fall Tour that I was invited to sing on the two and a half week Spring Tour. I was one of three guys that year awarded the opportunity to sing in both tours as a freshman. Some of my most memorable times are from being part of the men's chorus at Morehouse. Thank you to our director and all the brothers I sang with during my time in the glee club. You all taught me a lot, thank you!

I AM SEED:

I am doing the best I can.

6

HELP THE BEST YOU CAN

MY FIRST YEAR OF COLLEGE WAS TOUGH. It was such a drastic change. When I was in high school, I held down part time jobs and was "living the life." I was able to go around to different stores and shop when I wanted to, go to the movies with girls and (my absolute favorite thing to do) eat out whenever I desired. Coming to Morehouse, I didn't have the luxury of going to school at a set time and working all evenings and weekends like I had once before.

To anyone who has time to get an education and hold down any job, hats off to you because that is truly something difficult. In my first year experience, I didn't have time to work, and I didn't have the excess money to eat good food and shop. My parents were awesome. Whenever I needed money they would give me whatever they could, which I appreciated, but I always had stuff I wanted to buy. Coming to college, I learned to appreciate the small things at home that I didn't have in college: "free" laundry, parents providing hygiene materials, and who can forget the best part of being home—home cooked meals.

During my freshman year, all I ever ate was Pop-Tarts, assorted chips, and the ever-popular, awesomely delicious meal known as ramen noodles. The highlight of my week was Wednesday, because those were the days I would get the closest thing to a real meal. Anyone who attends an HBCU knows Wednesdays are the days the cafe serves fried chicken with mac 'n cheese and greens. It's the best thing ever! Other than that, most cafeteria food can be awful at times.

Frustrated by my discomfort, I reached out to my family to ask if we had any relatives close to Morehouse who could provide me with a taste of home life. I'll never forget calling my Aunt Christol. She is so connected and knows everything about everything. She told me I had family who resided in Lithonia, Georgia. At the time, I didn't know where Lithonia, Georgia was, but I knew I was making my way there to meet this family of mine. I was so excited to know that I had a potential break from regular days of ramen noodles and dorm snacks. I told my family to reach out immediately and connect me to these "Lithonians."

That next week I received a phone call from a woman who informed me that she was my distant aunt. Her name was Aunt Gwen. Our first conversation shocked me. I remember nervously answering the phone and hearing her soft, pleasant voice.

"Hello is this Christopher?" she asked.

"Yes!" I responded, knowing this was the family my aunt had informed me about. She was so pleasant. We talked for a good fifteen minutes. She kept telling me to give her a time and day and how she would arrange for someone to get me and take me to her home. It amazed me that someone I had never met was so interested in taking me in and taking care of me. For a while I was in disbelief; I thought it was too good to be true.

Sure enough, that next weekend I called Aunt Gwen, and she had her nephew pick me up. Aunt Gwen and I had only had two phone conversations ever, we never met in person, and here I was going to her home in Lithonia.

I remember riding in the car with her nephew. He told me about the family and asked me about college. It was a good conversation. The trip to her house was smooth because we had such a good conversation. Her nephew, whom I referred to as Cousin Jay, was a nice guy. He was almost as nice as Aunt Gwen. That car ride was about thirty minutes but it flew by. Jay kept telling me how nice Aunt Gwen was and how big her house was. I was so excited to get there.

When we arrived at Aunt Gwen's house, I was awestruck. Aunt Gwen had a private entrance and a gate around her estate. I had never experienced anything like it before. I instantly became nervous. Her house was gorgeous and sat in the center of acres of land. The house sat in the woods and was surrounded by beautiful trees and flowers. It was unlike anything I had ever seen in Ohio. When I got out of the car, I looked around and felt right at home. I walked up and humbly knocked on the door, wondering what kind of woman I would see on the other side. When the door opened, she was standing there with open arms asking for a hug.

"Hey, Christopher. Come on in, make yourself at home," she said to me with a big smile.

I instantly felt like I was home simply because she called me "Christopher." Since high school everyone has always called me: "Sumlin," "Chris-Sumlin" (one word) or only just, well, "Chris." "Christopher" has this intimate, family feel to it. Whenever I hear someone call me that it makes me feel close and relatable. My mother always calls me "Christopher." It's the best way to make me feel comfortable.

As I made my way through Aunt Gwen's home, it was beautiful. She had pictures of generations of family all over her walls. I saw pictures of her, her mother and all of the grandchildren. Her house truly felt like a home.

"Are you hungry?" she asked.

I had just come from the cafeteria before Jay came to get me from campus. I didn't know what to say. I didn't want to be rude or come off as pretentious.

"Well... I actually—" I said.

"Great! Say no more," she interrupted.

"Take your things downstairs. I am frying fish and it will be ready soon."

I was still lost and didn't know what to do so I did as I was told. I figured this was that southern hospitality I had heard so much about on TV. Jay was still with me, and we went downstairs to what was like a theater room. There was a big flat screen television and movies everywhere. I instantly felt even more comfortable.

Fifteen minutes passed and down came Aunt Gwen with a tray consisting of fried fish, vegetables, and rice. I was so happy I could have cried because I knew I was finally about to have some home cooked food.

"Need anything to drink?" she asked. "Let me grab you some juice and hot sauce for that fish."

Two seconds later she came back down with two more fillets of fish, juice, and my favorite hot sauce.

Boy, I tell you, that fish was so dang good. It was the kind of fish that sort of sizzles and dissolves in your mouth when you eat it. It was seasoned to perfection. I couldn't have been happier. Here I was in a beautiful home, with an amazing new relative, eating some fried fish that would make an atheist say, "Thank you, Jesus." I was in bliss.

That was a Friday night, and she told me I could stay the weekend, so of course I stayed Saturday night, and even stayed Sunday.

On Saturday after another home cooked meal, this time, breakfast, I got to talk to Aunt Gwen and get to know her. We had a heartfelt conversation about family, friendship and life. After much speculation, I couldn't help but ask her, "Aunt Gwen, why are you so nice to me? You just met me and here you are taking me into your home, treating me like royalty and loving me as if I were your own son. Why?"

Her response was something that has stuck with me to this day.

She looked me in my eyes and said, "Christopher, God has been good to me. He's brought me a long way. I owe it to him to give in every capacity I can. God always does right by good people, so always remember to be good."

Aunt Gwen is a very passionate person; she spoke with so much conviction. When she said that last statement her words hit me like a ton of bricks. Those words resonated with me greatly and made me think hard about life. She went on to say how she loved helping people, especially those who are trying to help themselves. She challenged me to always be good and help others where I can, no matter what happens with my life, career and future.

Of all the life lessons I have learned, this is one of my favorite lessons. I call this one, help the best you can. So many times while we are so busy dealing with life we cross paths with people who have needs. These needs may be financial, emotional or even spiritual. Sometimes we can get so caught up in all that is happening in our lives that we forget to help others along the way. Always do your best to help others because you never know the effect you can have on people. Aunt Gwen had no idea how homesick I felt and how badly I craved a good meal. She didn't know what I was eating in school and the emotional impact that all the changes of college had on me. By her opening her home, inviting me in and treating me as family, it made a world of difference in my life at that time. Her selflessness, generosity, and love made me feel so much better. She left an impact on my life that I will never forget.

I believe we all have that power. We all have the means and resources to not just make an impression on people, but an impact. Some of us are good listeners who can be a soothing ear, able to listen to anyone going through something. Some of us have the ability to give our time to help others reach their dreams. Some people even have it like Oprah, and can revolutionize education in Africa and build an entire school. We can't do everything, but we all can do something.

While you're reading this book, I challenge you to get still and really think hard about your life. I encourage you to look at your life and ask yourself, what can I do to brighten the days of those I encounter? What can your life do to serve others? When giving, make sure that it comes from an honest, genuine place. You may find it in your heart to say good morning and smile at everyone you see the next day. You may write a thank you letter that makes your boss or teacher smile. You may even buy your mom something nice just because. Whatever you do to help, do it well. Help with whatever you can. If we all did our part to compassionately help others with what we have, this world would be a better place. It all starts with you—go out there and help others, and I promise you may get more from giving than receiving.

After that breakfast at Aunt Gwen's, she took me shopping for dorm snacks—all funded by her. She loaded me down with more chips, candy, and water than I could ever imagine. Thank you, Aunt Gwen, for your love, support and kindness. I have never met someone so compassionate and loving. You taught me a valuable lesson about giving simply because it is good! I will never be able to repay you for the impact you had on me. I love you dearly.

I AM SEED:

I am doing my best to help those around me.

7

LET IT GO

I HAVE FAILED A LOT IN MY LIFE. I can say with confidence that I have failed more than I have succeeded. There were many times when I interviewed for jobs and did not get them. There were scholarships I applied for that I did not receive. There have been more girls I have liked than those who have liked me. If I got stuck on all of the times I have failed and not succeeded I would not be where I am or who I am today. I know for sure I would not have applied to Morehouse, applied for different jobs or even have written this book if I got so caught up in my past and failures.

Getting so distracted and immersed in the past is not a healthy space in which to live. It is hard to deal with what is in front of you if you continue to look at what is behind you. This is one of the lessons I continue to struggle with on a daily basis. Failure is something that I always encounter. Whenever I fail I make it a priority to pick myself back up, let it go and move on. No matter how big of a failure life presents you with, always remember to let it go. This lesson's hard, I know. But I promise if you let it go, pick yourself back up and move on you will be okay. No story or moment taught me this lesson better than my first-semester experience at Morehouse.

My first semester at Morehouse was such a challenge. I had a hard time adapting to all the new changes and difficulties that came with going to college. The level of academic rigor at Morehouse was far greater than that of high school. I came to Morehouse thinking that with the skills and endurance I gained from earning my associates in high school I would be just fine at Morehouse. This confidence became internal arrogance. There were nights sitting in the dorm when I knew I should have been studying, but I would push studying off to hang with my brothers throughout the dorm. I would spend my nights going from room to room, floor to floor, talking to any and everyone instead of doing my homework. I also enjoyed partying and turning up. I had the perspective that I was free and could do whatever I wanted now that I was in college.

I was so busy being a socialite that my grades suffered tremendously. I remember going to class every day but not putting in the necessary time outside of class to succeed. By the time midterm grades were released, I was in a rut. When I went to check my grades at the end of the semester my report was filled with poor grades and not a single A was in sight. I was deeply disappointed and ashamed. I knew that I was capable of more, but for some reason I simply just was not focused. I was too busy making friends, turning up and hanging around in the dorm. It was not fun sitting at home during winter break knowing that I had poor grades. As grades started pouring in for everyone, a lot of guys in my class posted their grades to social media. As I scrolled my timelines, I saw guys who sat right next to me in the class post about their 3.5 and 3.8 GPAs. It was such a reality shock to know the same guys I ate with, laughed with and even had partied with, still managed to succeed in their classes. Seeing all of their success made me feel like such a failure and a loser. After a while, I took a break from social media. I did not want to talk to anyone about school. I was so hard on myself for failing and not putting my academics first.

For the rest of winter break, I had no confidence at all. All of my friends back home in Ohio wanted to meet up and ask about how my first semester at Morehouse was, but I had no interest in talking. I saw myself as a failure and a fraud. I just knew I was ready to get back to school and redeem myself.

After a long and pitiful winter break, it was finally time for the spring semester. I was on fire. I picked myself up and told myself that last semester did not matter and that this semester was a new beginning. When I walked into my dorm building for the second time in January, I was so excited. I was ready to get the semester going and just do my thing. When I walked into the building I was smiling from ear to ear with my luggage in-hand. As I began to make my way up the stairs I saw a bulletin board that read, "YOU COULD HAVE A 4.0 BUT YOU'RE PLAYING." The bulletin board took everyone's GPAs in the building and posted them without the names so everyone could see where we all stood as brothers. Looking at the board I saw four perfect 4.0s, I saw a couple of 3.5s, I saw some 3.8s. It seemed as if everyone had a good semester except me.

Instantly all my shame and guilt came back. I saw my low GPA on the bulletin board in the corner. I am still so ashamed of it I don't even want to mention it in this book. Just know that it was bad. I saw my GPA and completely felt that it defined me. All I could think of was all the tests I failed, all the assignments I could have done better on. It was a rough moment I won't forget. After about thirty minutes of standing there ruminating over my previous semester, I picked up my belongings and went upstairs to my room. My freshman year I lived on the fourth floor of the building, and it was a long walk taking my luggage up to the fourth floor of that building. With every step up those stairs I kept telling myself, "It is okay, people fail. You will do better next time, push onward."

That moment helped me get through the first few weeks of the semester. I was doing pretty well mentally until we had the Annual Morehouse Scholar's Day.

Scholar's Day is the one day out of the year when Morehouse honors students who've achieved academic excellence in a school-wide assembly. It was an interesting day. Of course, I was in the glee club my freshman year, so I was required to attend, be attentive and on stage as the ceremony was in process. We had to sing that morning. I remember we sang a hymnal called "Ascribe to the Lord." That assembly is another freshman year moment I will never forget. Oddly, it was the emptiest assembly I had ever been to my freshman year. It seemed as if half the student body just decided not to show up. I can only imagine what some of my other brothers were feeling that morning. I am sure they probably felt some of the same insecurities and shame I felt that day and decided simply not to attend the assembly. Nonetheless I was there, suited and booted and on the stage.

As I sat on stage with the men's chorus, I flipped through the pages of the program only to find that my name was not on the Dean's List. Of course, I wasn't surprised, but at that moment it hit me like a boulder. Again I felt like a failure; my self-esteem was shot. I didn't understand how I could attend the school of my dreams and not do what I came there to do. To add to my shame, my roommate Douglas earned a perfect 4.0 that semester. Of all the conversations and hanging we did in the room, I never knew that Douglas was doing that well in his classes. I was astonished that the man living next to me faced the same challenges I did and still succeeded so much more. I knew that I wanted to learn from him and see how he was able to earn a 4.0.

That night Douglas and I had a great conversation about our goals, our futures and what mattered. I gained a lot of respect for Douglas that night. I kept complimenting him on how big of a deal it was that he earned a 4.0, but he was so humble. I told him my story and how ashamed I was that I didn't do that well. Douglas was understanding but stern. He said how smart he knew I was and how I just needed to get focused and get serious.

Hearing someone I admired and looked up to remind me of who I was relieved me of all the shame I had been feeling. Douglas never told me I was a failure or that I was not smart, he just kept reiterating the fact that I was intelligent and talented. I believe that in that moment I let go of my failure and saw myself differently. I no longer identified with my failure past or even my low GPA. That day I truly let go of my past.

Sometimes when dealing with life, we beat ourselves up over the past and let it break us down. After failing many assignments and making poor grades, again I was devastated. I let my failure define myself to the point where I completely lost my self-esteem. I didn't want to apply for jobs; I didn't want to tell people I went to Morehouse; I didn't even want to return. After my freshman year I thought, "Maybe I'm not built for college. Maybe high school was my peak." It is so crazy how often we let our history define our destiny. As you read this book and hear this story, I just want to remind you to always remember that in life things happen. We fail, we cry, and we make mistakes, but it is all part of a bigger perfect plan for our lives.

My freshman year I was still adapting and trying to figure myself out. If I could go back and change the situation I would have worked a lot harder academically and handled my business, but I simply can't. I can't go back to that time in my life and change what's already done. It is in the past. The only thing I can do is pick myself up and learn from the situation.

From that experience, I learned a valuable lesson. I learned better how to balance academics and social life. I learned that I didn't want to feel ashamed of my grades when others asked. I learned that if I wanted to succeed I would have to work hard.

Maybe you have great grades or don't have a mistake so easy to fix. Maybe you had a child young, ruined your credit at an early age or entertained a bad relationship. I am here to tell you that it is okay. We all have a past and have made mistakes of which we are ashamed to remind ourselves. The only thing we can do with the past is to learn from it and grow. Don't ever let your history deny you your destiny. When you fall, dust yourself off and get back to going. When you're trying to do anything in life, failure is inevitable. If you meet someone who hasn't had to deal with failure, I'm certain they probably haven't done anything of value either.

The next year I did, in fact, return to Morehouse, and I made the Dean's List. That year I had the confidence to keep going. I understood that even though I had a rough start, I would have a better ending. That's the mindset you have to have. Don't beat yourself up over your past; it's all a part of creating your epic story! Keep going, keep the faith and remember, never let your history deter you from your destiny—just let it go.

I AM SEED:

I am letting go of my history because of my epic destiny.

8

DARING DECISIONS

I believe there is a real supreme power in making a decision. Think about the last time you were asked a question and you definitively said "no" or "yes." Reflect on how much power lay in your decision. When dealing with life, we are faced with so many options, questions, and choices. These are things that we cannot escape. As soon as we wake up in the morning we are faced with a plethora of decisions we must make. These decisions can be as simple as: What am I going to wear today? Will I go to class? Will I call my mother? Will I go to work? There are so many questions in our lives. These questions give us so much power and influence in our lives. Think about how many times someone has looked at you and said, "You decide, this is up to you." I am sure you felt empowered and pressured to make a decision that was in the best interest of everyone. Sometimes when we decide to take a chance and make a daring decision we create some of our most memorable moments.

I met the actor Jussie Smollett in the spring of 2015 because I made a daring decision, and that day became one I will never forget.

It was a beautiful day in Atlanta. It was also the day of UNCF's An Evening of Stars Charity Gala. This event is one that took place in Atlanta's Civic Center. It is a very prestigious and grand event. There are enormous lights and projectors everywhere; everyone gets all dressed up in their Sunday best, all for one cause—supporting The United Negro College Fund. This was my second time attending, and I wanted to have a good time. It all started with my outfit. Of course, I wanted to look good because when you look good, you feel good. I wore a Morehouse button-up that had the Morehouse "M" logo imprinted into the sleeve. I had a nice navy blue blazer, great slacks, and a good brown shoe. I felt so confident and good.

After getting dressed, I walked tall and proud and went to get my good friend Randall Smith.

Randall is easily the funniest and most confident person I have ever met. No matter where he is, Randall always puts on a good show and makes everyone around him laugh. It was only right that I went to the event with him because I knew we would have a good time.

I remember we did not have a way to get to the event, so I had to order an Uber. Of course, it was a Gala and Randall, and I felt it was appropriate to order a Suburban. We felt that no matter how much money we had, or who saw us, we deserved to ride around in a Suburban because of how good we looked.

As I was in the SUV, I sent my friend who had our tickets a text message. I had received tickets from a friend who got me tickets to the event because I was a UNCF Scholarship recipient. She told me I would get two tickets, but I had no idea where they were. After riding around Atlanta in the Suburban and feeling all fresh, we arrived at the venue. I quickly saw my friend and she looked discouraged and disappointed. I asked her what was wrong, and she informed me that the tickets I was receiving were at the very back of the balcony. I'm a humble guy, I had no problem with sitting in the back, but Randall felt otherwise.

When I told Randall what had happened, he looked at me and said, "Sumlin, I do not know about you, but a star like me doesn't sit just anywhere in an event."

I was so shocked at his level of confidence. Randall just knew that we were not sitting in the back of this event. As we stood there outside of the event, we discussed what we would do to get to the lower deck of the event. Randall was so serious; he was not playing any games. After ten minutes went by we began admiring the red carpet that was to our left. Randall looked at me and said again, "Sumlin, watch this. I am about to go pump on this red carpet."

For those of you reading this who are not familiar with the southern lingo, "pump" is a word used to describe a strong, confident walk. I didn't believe him. There were cameras everywhere, and people all over. I knew I wasn't invited onto the red carpet, so I was just waiting to see what Randall was going to do.

Sure enough, I looked to my right for two seconds, and the next thing

I know Randall somehow made his way over to the red carpet and was walking through the carpet taking pictures. It was hilarious. Something you had to see. Of course I didn't make that decision; I made the decision to stay left behind. Randall went through the entire red carpet in about three minutes.

After seeing him enter the building, I quickly called him and yelled, "Randall, what are you doing? How dare you just jump on that carpet and walk?"

He said, "Sumlin, when the Spirit says move, you gotta move." And he hung up the phone. I could not help but laugh, knowing that it was not any "spirit" that convinced him to break the rules and walk on the red carpet. I strongly believe that everyone on the carpet probably knew that Randall didn't belong on the red carpet, but with his confidence who would dare to stop him?

Because I made the decision to stay where I was, I humbly went through the security gate and proceeded into the area in the same manner that the rest of the general public went in. Shortly after running around the building I ran back into Randall. I asked him what we were going to do about our ticket situation. He proclaimed, "Sumlin, just walk down there and tell them you belong on the floor. They won't know any better."

This time, I got tired of Randall having all of the confidence and it began to rub off on me. I straightened my back out, stuck my chest out and said, "You know what? You're right. I will just walk down there and let them know The Chris Sumlin is a star and he does not sit in anyone's balcony." I felt strong and ready for action; I think my bladder felt it too because

I sure did need to urinate after I made that proclamation. After finishing my business in the bathroom, I had the balcony ticket in my hand. I was in that stall for a good ten minutes as my mind began to race.

After much reflection and thought I took the ticket that was given to me in the balcony and flushed it down the toilet. I made the choice that I was not sitting in the balcony, and I would find a way to sit closer. It was like a scene in a movie, very empowering and, well...dramatic. The toilet was very nice and new—that drain got rid of that ticket so fast, it was something to see. Following the bathroom episode, I went back out to the auditorium where guests were still finding their seats. I found an usher who was seating people in the front of the auditorium.

So there I was in my good outfit and confidence, ready to make my way to the floor seating.

I went to the usher and said confidently, "Hi, excuse me. I'm supposed to sit in the front on the floor."

"Do you have a ticket?" she asked.

"No, I was given the wrong one, so I gave it away. Is there any way you can find me another one?" I replied.

By the look on her face, I could tell she knew something wasn't right, but she went along with it. I was very bold and spoke with conviction. I made the choice that the floor was where I was supposed to be. I could tell the usher felt my energy.

"Hold on," she instructed.

She later came back and stated, "Down here is where there will be lots of seat fillers. We will be fluctuating fillers in and out of the auditorium during the production to make sure it looks full. I can get you a filler seat right in the front if that is okay."

"That would be perfect," I said confidently.

She escorted me down to the fourth row of the event. I was so happy and relieved I didn't have to sit in the balcony. All I could do was look up towards the balcony and say, "Thank God I'm not up there." I knew that had it not been for my decision making and me believing in myself, that usher would have kicked me straight out of the event.

Shortly after our interaction, the Evening of Stars event began. It was dark, and the crowd started to applaud. As people were clapping, Mr. Jussie Smollett came and sat right in front of me. I was in awe. I was amazed I was again this close to a TV star. During the event we shared a couple of jokes and laughs, and then he asked me for my cell phone.

"Hey man, quickly throw me your phone. Let's take a selfie."

Of course I agreed and BOOM! There it was, a picture with Jussie Smollett. The rest of the night was an amazing experience. I had such a great time and had an amazing seat. Throughout the evening I could not help but think how things would have been, had I settled for my ticket and sat in the balcony. I probably wouldn't have had a good time and definitely would not have gotten my selfie with one of today's biggest television stars.

After that experience, I knew that life was all about choices. I firmly believe in the three Cs of life: Choice, Chance, and Change. In life we must make the choice to take the chance if we want to get a change. It is just that simple. I did not know if that usher would accommodate me and allow me to sit in the front of the auditorium. Yet, I still made the choice to take the chance. In life, just decide! Decide what you want to do, make the choice to make it happen and let every step you take move you into the direction of your dreams. Now, I am not advising you to flush your tickets to events down the toilet and do what I did in that moment. But you can apply the principle of action-decision making to many aspects of your life.

If you want to go to college, sign up and go. If you would love to be in shape and fit into a certain pants size, then implement the proper diet and exercise and go for it. I believe we all have the capacity to reach for our dreams. All it takes is making the choice to own that power. You can do it. You are excellent. You are brilliant. You could be doing a million things right now, but you chose to sit here and read a book about dealing with life. You have what it takes to do something great. Just make the decision and go for it! Dare greatly! You never know what making one big decision can lead to in your life. I promise you, you definitely know what will happen if you don't make a decision—nothing. There's a quote that says, "The cost of inaction is far greater than the cost of making a mistake."

Imagine if Beyoncé never made the decision to sing. Imagine if Barack Obama never made the decision to run for president. When dealing with life, of course everyone is going to have obstacles, but that is no excuse not to step out of faith and make some daring decisions. Go out there in the world, make some awesome decisions and do your thing! You deserve it! And if no one believes in you, I do, simply because I know it works.

Thank you, Randall, for giving me that confidence to give myself permission to be an action-decision maker. You influenced me to decide that I was not going to take that seat, but instead take a chance to find something better. I appreciate you and your crazy ways.

I AM SEED:

I am a daring decision maker.

9

GET IN THE GAME

I USED TO BE ONE OF THOSE PEOPLE who wanted to be liked by everyone. I would go out of my way to make sure I was liked and respected. This took a lot of energy, and finally, I decided to focus on myself. I knew that it was impossible for me to be led by the opinions of others and be successful at the same time. If you, or someone you know, wants to be successful but has the disease to please, tell them it will not happen. You cannot be great and give life your all while being oppressed by what people think of you. If you haven't heard, criticism is inevitable. When you are dealing with life, always remember to have tough skin and not be overly sensitive to what others say about you. This is a hard practice because by nature we all want to feel accepted, validated and be liked. In no way am I encouraging you to become so cocky and heartless that you only care about yourself and have no compassion for others. I am merely stating that when dealing with life, there will be times when people who don't know you, or even like you, will criticize you for no real reason. These are what you call haters.

We all have haters. We all have people in our lives that may not like us simply because of who we are.

I say all this to say, it is important always to keep ignoring negativity. If you have big goals and ambitions, keep those first. Do not worry about what other people say about you—do your thing, stay strong and forget the haters. I had a physics class that taught me this lesson more than ever.

My sophomore year at Morehouse I took an Introduction to Physical Science class that was really a headache. I hate physics; it is truly one of the worst classes I have ever taken. It was one of those classes where I had to actually read the textbook over and over again to really understand the lessons. I will never forget this physics class. The class was so packed. The classroom could probably fit about fifty guys in it, and I estimate there were probably forty-eight guys in the class. There were so many personalities in the class, and the professor was not a fan favorite. His name was Professor Eddie Red, and he challenged us like you wouldn't even imagine. Professor Red hardly ever canceled class, and he gave us lots of assignments and quizzes. He really is a great professor, one who will make sure you get your money's worth.

In his class, I was always the one who had a lot of the questions. I knew that I had trouble learning physics, so I always made sure I asked questions. Although I was happy and comfortable asking questions, some of my other Morehouse brothers were less pleased with my persistent question asking.

One day we were in class learning about heat and temperature. Professor Red was teaching, and I was so confused. In retrospect, Professor Red was actually doing his job well, but I didn't read the chapter that week, so of course it was harder for me to grasp what was being taught. As he continued to lecture, I heard three guys complain about how bad our professor was doing and how they didn't understand anything he was teaching. Me being me, I leaned into the conversation and asked, "Did you guys do the reading? All of his examples come directly from the book."

One of the guys turned to me and said, "No, I didn't read that mess."

After that, I knew then that this was why none of us could understand what was being taught.

Time went by, and after the concept had been explained Professor Red asked us if we had any questions. I knew that I had needed to do the reading, but I still thought it was better to try and learn rather than to stay silent and ignorant. After he asked the class for questions, I quickly and confidently raised my hand and said, "Professor, do you mind if I come down there and do a problem with you? I kind of understand what is going on, but I need just a little more help. Do you mind helping me?"

My heart was racing so fast because I knew if he did say yes, I would have to go down in front of this big group of guys and learn this hard stuff with the risk of embarrassing myself. On the other hand, if he said no, then I would be even more embarrassed because here I was putting myself out there, and I would have hated to be rejected. I figured there was no way I could win. As my heart was racing, and I awaited his answer, Professor Red chuckled and said, "Yes, Mr. Sumlin! Come on down and we can work on this problem together."

I felt a breath of release as I knew that this was an opportunity to learn something I didn't know already. I was honestly nervous because of how large the room was.

The class was so large, and there were lots of seats in the room. All of the seats were on an incline up towards the wall; the room was set up like bleachers at a baseball game. If you were sitting in the last row, you would be at the very top of the room looking down to the professor. That day I came in late, and so I was at the very top of the room, in the last row. I knew this was a moment I would regret later.

I did not have time to keep thinking about what it was I had just done. By this time the entire class was looking at me, ready to see if I was actually going to walk down to the professor to do this problem. Professor Red was patiently waiting too, as all of these thoughts were going through my head. I knew I had to go down there, so I made sure my shirt was tucked in, grabbed my book, pad, and pen and walked down to the front of the room.

As I was walking down those long stairs, I heard people laughing at me, calling me names such as "suck up," "teacher's pet" and "know it all." I'd be lying if I said those comments didn't faze me, but I knew that I could not entertain that negative energy and that I had every right to go down there and do this problem.

Luckily, the example problem I did with Professor Red was actually quite simple. We did a problem that exemplified the first law of thermodynamics.

After I was done, the professor told me I did a good job, and I proudly went back to my seat. As I walked back up those long stairs, those same guys who were laughing at me when I walked down the stairs were asking the professor to do another problem because they still did not "get it." Once class was over, I was called to the professor's office, and we discussed today's class.

I expressed how today's class was not the only class in which I felt that I was being picked on for engaging in class. Professor Red was a good guy, a Morehouse man to be exact. He told me how good it was that I put myself out there and tried to learn.

He told me, "Always remember to keep the main thing, the main thing." At first, I did not quite understand what he was saying, but after I had repeated those words a few times, his advice made sense. I call it the "Get in the Game" principle.

When dealing with life, there will always be naysayers. There are always going to be people who mean you no good, want to destroy you or see you fall flat on your face. The important thing to do is to get in the game and play anyway. Of course, I do not mean an actual game, I mean this figuratively.

Here are two examples:

Imagine you're at school, and your main priority is to get good grades and pass. That's the game you're playing, the game of making good grades and passing. Do everything in your power to keep that priority first. Never let someone's approval steer you away from your goal. If you're at work and you are excellent at your job, someone may get jealous. Stay strong and don't let what they say or do affect you. You are there to make money and do your job to the best of your ability. You are in the game of doing your job, not in the game of making friends.

Whenever I face opposition or receive senseless criticism, I get still and think really hard. I ask myself, "What is my true intention? What is my top priority in what it is I am trying to do?"

When you know your intentions and priorities, no one can stop you. The "Get in the Game" principle is really about knowing what it is you are trying to accomplish, and having the confidence that you have it in you to do so.

When I was walking down those stairs to do the problem with Professor Red, of course I was nervous, of course I was insecure and doubtful, but I kept walking. I understood that my priority was to learn and do well in physics. I did not let the negativity from those guys in that class restrain me from getting my education.

It is kind of like basketball. I will never forget watching the 2015 NBA Finals. It was the Cleveland Cavaliers vs. the Golden State Warriors. I am from Ohio, so of course I was rooting for LeBron James and the Cavs. I enjoyed watching the Cavs play, and I thought LeBron was doing an excellent job. He was running up and down the court, making every shot he could and doing what he does best. Unfortunately, when I read social media people felt otherwise. So many people had everything negative to say about LeBron—why he wasn't a good enough player and what he could have done better—it was bad. I even saw some of the Golden State fans at the arena giving LeBron a hard time. I am sure that LeBron James was aware of the negativity, but no matter what, LeBron kept lacing up his shoes, wiping his brow and playing all the way until the end of the game.

The truth is, the people in the stands are just that, in the stands. At the end of the day, it was LeBron James who was the man of the hour; he had to play those NBA Final games. How unfortunate would it have been if every time LeBron heard a negative comment from the crowd he dropped, stopped playing and went home? I am sure a lot more people would have been disappointed.

I say all of this to say, never allow yourself to be too affected by criticism and haters. Get in the game when times are tough and everyone isn't cheering your name. Whether it be a basketball game you are playing, a presentation you are giving, or you are singing in a concert, always remember to get in the game.

Following that class, I continued to raise my hand in class, participate and do the readings. Professor Red came to be very impressed with me. He told me I should consider being a teacher because I seemed very natural in front of the class. He even advised me to hold study sessions for the brothers in that class because our class average was not as high as he had liked it to be. By the second exam, I became the unofficial physics tutor for our class. I ended up earning an A in that class, and some of those same guys who were laughing at me when I went to do that problem the first time were some of my most regular attendees at the study sessions I held.

Thank you so much, Professor Red for allowing me to come down in front of the class and work out that problem with you. Because of that moment, I learned a valuable lesson about getting in the game no matter what. Thank you!

I AM SEED:

I am getting in the game no matter who is in the stands.

10

THE POWER
OF COLLABORATION

FRIENDSHIP AND COLLABORATION are two of life's essential joys. Often, especially among young men, we are afraid to open up and work together with others. In reality, we all need help. I heard a quote once that said, "If you want to go fast go alone, but if you want to go far go with others." I feel that when you have friends to collaborate with, it is easier to accomplish goals. No adventure or story will better embody the importance of collaboration than the story of how I met the singer Rihanna.

One Thursday, I saw a post online about Rihanna hosting a meet-and-greet at a mall in Atlanta. Immediately, I knew I had to meet her. My family and I have been Rihanna fans for years. A lot of her songs were background music on Saturdays when we would clean the house. There was even one point when my father swore he was going to sing "Take A Bow" at church because of its empowering message. He loved the, "but it's over now" line.

Rihanna has been part of my life for some time. Upon hearing of this meet and greet, I thought to myself, "How cool would it be to say I met such a big superstar like Rihanna?" I found the store phone number, called the store and asked the manager for details about the event. The manager expressed that to meet Rihanna, I had to buy the singer's fragrance because the event was being held as a promotional event for her new men's fragrance. When I heard this information, I became worried. As a college student, I don't have a lot of money, and the money I have goes to essentials like laundry, hygiene materials, and books.

Hesitantly I asked, "So how much does the fragrance cost?" I held my breath and waited for the answer.

The manager said, "The gift package costs sixty-nine ninety-nine plus tax."

When I heard these words, my heart dropped. I thought, "How am I supposed to get the money for this cologne?" At the time, I only had a hundred dollars to last for the entire week. I had to budget for transportation to and from the mall and snacks in case I got hungry.

When my mind began to race, I came to the conclusion that I would have to ask a friend to go with me, and we would split the cost of everything equally. This way the financial load would be lifted, and I'd have a friend to share the experience with. I thought, who wouldn't want to stand in line with a good friend to crack jokes and laugh together while you wait? Everyone, right? The question was who that friend would be.

Following that phone conversation, I went into my dorm room and there was my roommate, Corbin. Corbin and I had just become roommates, and we weren't really that close before living together. Corbin was busy watching basketball highlights, decompressing from the long day. I had just come in from my last class. It was late in the afternoon. As I began to think more about the excitement of meeting Rihanna, I knew Corbin would be the best collaborator to go on this adventure. I was a little apprehensive to ask if he'd be willing to do this with me, but I thought he might be down for the cause.

I knew that if I were to ask him, I should be considerate and talk to him in a casual manner. After a long day of classes, no one wants to be asked more questions in their down time. To begin, I asked him about his day, how were classes going and all this other stuff to break the ice. He seemed in good spirits, as if he had a good day, so I slid in the big question.

"So, Corbin, would you like to meet Rihanna with me this weekend?"

After I asked the question, I just sat there across the room, looking at him with a smile. I expected an immediate reaction, but to my surprise, he just looked at me without saying a word. You would think most people would be overly excited to meet Rihanna, but not this guy. Corbin's a sports enthusiast; I am sure he probably couldn't name five Rihanna songs if his life counted on it. I knew at this moment I had to push for a yes and try to convince him to go.

With a big smile, I added, "It would be so much fun. Just think about all the people who would love to see you with such a big celebrity. You'd get so many Facebook likes." He still didn't say a word. I began to lose hope.

As he sat there contemplating he finally looked up and said, "Do you think I'll be able to grab her ass?"

After that question, I immediately wanted to laugh, but I knew this was my point of leverage that I had to talk up.

"Yeah, man. If we play it right I think you'll be able to pull that off. Sure, why not?" I said with false confidence.

"Alright, I'm in. So what all do we have to do?"

I knew that I had gotten far with him since he'd agreed to go, but this is when I suspected he would lose all interest. I thought to myself how much I was counting on this guy. He already wasn't too pumped about going; now he has to spend money too. This is it. Hesitantly I sat down and expressed the big catch of the entire event by stating, "Umm... Well... The meet and greet is a promotional event for a men's cologne she is pushing. The meet and greet is on Saturday, but to get a picture with her, we have to buy the cologne and get a ticket tomorrow morning."

As I looked at Corbin, I noticed how much he was chilling. He is a very chill, relaxed guy, but he really was relaxed. I wasn't sure that he was listening until Corbin asked me, "Well, how much does it run for?"

"It's about seventy dollars, and we would have to pay for transportation to and from. You in?"

Corbin again asked, "Do you really think I will be able to grab her ass?"

"Yeah, man. Just go for it," I said. I prayed Corbin was joking. I pictured him trying to grab Rihanna, succeeding and getting escorted straight out.

After some thinking, Corbin finally said, "Alright, I'm in." With that, I collaborated with Corbin, we had a plan to meet Rihanna, and I had someone to help me fund my adventure.

That Thursday night we strategized about how we would get to the mall the next morning to buy the cologne. We agreed that I would pay for the trip to the mall, Corbin would pay for the journey back, and we would come back to Morehouse and eat in the cafeteria. We also planned to get to the mall early in the morning so we could have the chance to buy the cologne before the store ran out. Corbin suggested we get to the mall around six in the morning because the shop opened at eight.

I watched all my Thursday night favorite shows, and both of us were asleep by 11:00 p.m. Anyone in college who lives on campus knows how early this is, but we were determined.

The next morning my alarm went off at 5:30 a.m. and it was a struggle for me to get up. I wanted more sleep and knew it would be a long day. I could only imagine how tired Corbin would feel, and after hitting my snooze button I looked across the room to see if he was awake.

"Corbin, you up?" I asked in a dreadful tone from exhaustion.

Before I could even blink, Corbin immediately jumped up, grabbed his toothbrush and headed to brush his teeth and get the day going. At this moment, I thanked God for a good friend to collaborate with, because if it had been just me, I probably would have rolled over and gone back to sleep.

Before we knew it, we were all washed up, dressed and on our way. As we agreed, I paid for the taxi there, and we finally made it to the mall. It was a chilly, dark Friday morning. We arrived approximately around 6:30 a.m. When we arrived, there were about ten people in line. Everyone was so excited. It was cold and dark yet fun. Fifteen minutes into our wait, a van of security officers pulled up to the building. They instructed all of us who were waiting outside the store to leave the area because it was too early and no one was allowed that close to the store before opening. At that moment I was nervous, and my mind began to fill with questions like where would I go, what would I do, and how could I make the time pass quickly. All the other fans who were waiting with their friends got into their cars and drove away. I knew that I had caught a cab and had no car, so what was I to do? Standing there stuck, Corbin called me over and asked what our next move would be. That very minute my fear subsided because I remembered I had a friend to hang with. I had forgotten that, unlike most times, this time I was not alone. I was so grateful that I asked this brother to come along with me. If I had experienced this wait alone it would have been dreadful, but because I had a friend with me it was cool. Corbin and I moved to another parking lot across from the store where the cologne was being sold. It was cold, both of our noses were running, and it was so early, but none of that mattered.

As we waited in the parking lot, it was fun. We were just hanging, talking about school and cracking jokes. The wait for the store to open ended up being a good experience. Time went by very fast. Before I knew it, it was 8:00 a.m., the store was open, and we were allowed to purchase the cologne. Corbin and I were some of the first people in the line. We both bought the cologne separately, got our passes to meet Rihanna and headed back to campus. With our cologne and passes in-hand, we rushed back to Morehouse because we both had classes that morning. I remember that Friday being a regular day as if nothing unusual had happened that morning. Saturday was the big day when Rihanna was going to be at the mall, and I was beyond excited.

That night, I fell asleep watching every Rihanna interview and music video I could find to hype myself up to meet her. That Saturday morning, I woke up relaxed but excited. The hard part was getting the cologne and the ticket to be able to participate in the meet and greet. Waking up that morning I was relaxed because I knew for a fact that I was going to see Rihanna and get my picture because I had my ticket.

Corbin and I got dressed, we grabbed our tickets, and again, we were on the run ready for day two of our Rihanna adventure. As we pulled up to the mall the parking lot was packed with cars. People were outside wrapped around the building waiting to meet Rihanna. However, the long line didn't bother me because I knew Corbin and I would clown with each other, have fun and make the most of the situation. We walked up to the waiting line area outside of the store and began to wait our turn. As we waited in line it was just like the morning before—we both cracked jokes, talked about whatever we could, and it was enjoyable. Funny thing was, all the girls around were giving Corbin the eyes and trying to flirt with him. At one point a girl looked at him and said, "Come on Trey Songz," as if Corbin were Trey himself. It was hilarious. Corbin loved the attention.

After waiting an hour, we were finally in the building, and we got to see Rihanna personally. She was taller than I anticipated and gorgeous. Due to there being so many people waiting, the line was built in a way that there were a lot of zig-zags and security gates. There was one point where we were waiting in line and Corbin and I were directly across from Rihanna. Everyone around us was crying, pouring their hearts out, and screaming her name. I'm a guy who loves attention, so I knew I had to do something to differentiate myself from everyone else and get her attention.

I had something in mind. As everyone was doing the most, I looked across the room at Rihanna, jumped in the air and screamed, "Rihanna!" in the most obnoxious, dramatic tone. Everyone around started laughing, hell, even I thought it was funny. As I collected myself, I looked up, and Rihanna was looking dead at me laughing too. It was one of my proudest moments.

Fifteen minutes later it was show time, and Corbin and I were up next to finally get our picture. I kept telling Corbin to go ahead of me and meet her first. I wanted to see how he reacted to her and then I would follow up in the same manner. Little did I know, Corbin had the same plan. We went back and forth about who should go first until the security guard motioned for me to step up to meet Rihanna. I'm sure after my scream he knew that I should be the one to go first. I was terrified, but I walked to her. As I was walking up to Rihanna, I was floored by how good she smelled. The perfume she wore was heavenly. I have never in my life smelled a woman who smelled so good. That scent would make Stevie Wonder take off his shades to see who that was. She was breathtaking. She stood tall in her black ensemble, long, straight black hair with a golden necklace that read "Fenty." Rihanna was looking so good! As I went up to her, I said, "Rihanna! Hey, sis." I gave her a warm hug. She was so sweet. After that, I said, "I love your song, 'Do Ya Thang.' It's one of my family's favorites."

"I love that song," Rihanna said in her thick Bajan accent.

"Yeah, girl. It should've gotten a video," I stated in a comedic tone, as if I had known her my whole life. Once again Rihanna laughed, and we embraced each other for our picture. My smile was as big as Texas. "Cheese," said the photographer. We took a picture together and that was the experience. It was over. Everything happened so quickly, but I loved every second of it. Corbin was in line next to meet Rihanna.

A lot was going on so I couldn't look back and observe Corbin's experience. Sadly, none of us will ever know what happened between Corbin and Rihanna, because when I asked Corbin what happened, he had no recollection of the experience at all. Still to this day I get on him about how he didn't grab her ass. I guess he was truly star struck, but hey, who could blame him? We went back to Morehouse that Saturday afternoon, excited to share our story with the brothers back on campus. After we both had posted our pictures to Facebook, everyone was contacting us to ask about the adventure. It was awesome.

The lesson I learned from this experience is to always be open to collaborating. Had it not been for Corbin, I would not have met Rihanna because I could not afford to commute to the mall for two days. It's great to have friends around who can help you achieve your goals, even personal goals that mattered to me and not Corbin.

We all need someone to pick us up when we are down, make us laugh when we want to cry or even stand with us in the line when we go to meet Rihanna. Remember that there would be no Kanye West if there was no Jay-Z. There would be no Destiny's Child if it were just Beyoncé. Michael Jackson would not have been a star without collaborating with his brothers as The Jackson 5. Always be open to working with others. Collaboration is a great thing, especially if you have someone cool to collaborate with. I advise you to find friends who share your goals and ambition. Surround yourself with people who force you to level up and will do whatever it takes to help you get to your goals. Nothing is more powerful than common people with a common goal.

Since then, Corbin has become one of my best friends. Corbin taught me many things, and we take pride in our friendship being based on collaboration and doing what Corbin calls "dope stuff." There are many things that I would not have accomplished had I not had someone to tag in when the match got tight. So go out there, make friends, and go for your goals as a team. And who knows, some of those same people you collaborate with could become your closest friends. Thanks, Corbin! You're the real MVP.

I AM SEED:

I am open to collaborating with others to achieve my dreams.

11

HOLD ON

I CAN SAY THAT MY GREATEST ACCOMPLISHMENT thus far has been interning out in Los Angeles in the summer of 2015. I had the time of my life out there, but very few people know the backstory of how I got to Los Angeles. I have to tell this story in this book; I would be careless if I didn't. My journey to Los Angeles taught me the benefits of truly holding on when life gets tough. This story is a great one, and one I still am amazed by to this day.

I will never forget the day I decided I want to go to Los Angeles to intern. The decision really just came to me. I can honestly say there was no pivotal moment, and no futuristic dream that I was walking down Hollywood Boulevard. One day I just felt it in my heart that Los Angeles was where I wanted to work during the summer of 2015.

For me Los Angeles represented uncharted territory. Growing up my life was Columbus, and I did not do much traveling. It was not until high school that I boarded my first flight. Thankfully, in college, I was blessed to travel up and down the east coast with the Morehouse College Glee Club, but never once had I ever been to Los Angeles.

One day I was in my dorm room, talking to Corbin. Classes were finished for the day, and we were in our dorm room watching TV. Nothing spectacular happened, but I just looked over at him and said, "I think I want to go to LA this summer and intern."

"Really?" he replied with deep curiosity.

"Yeah, I've never been out west, and just imagine all the experiences I would have there."

A few seconds went by.

"Hey, why not? I could see that for you," Corbin replied. "If anyone could do something great in Hollywood around here, it would be you."

By him affirming what I just suspected and agreeing with what I said, I felt validated. I felt maybe I could just make this happen. I often hear folks say, "Don't tell your big dreams to people because they will shoot them down."

But what an honor it is when you have people in your life who believe in your dreams as much, if not more than, you do. If you have someone like that in your life, cherish them, because that is a real treasure.

After that small conversation with Corbin, a fire in me was lit. All I could think about for the rest of the night was Los Angeles. I told myself that whatever it took I was going to be in Los Angeles interning that summer.

The next day, I began doing as much research as I could on Los Angeles. I wanted to know how big the city was, what companies were out there and how much housing ran. I had always heard people say that the cost of living on the west side was high, but I never knew just how high they were talking.

The apartments I looked at were more than house payments in Ohio. I saw studio apartments in Hollywood for $3,200. I saw a bedroom rental posting online for $1,800 a month. At one point I got excited because I saw a posting for discounted housing for college students. Little did I know it was housing near Beverly Hills, and the rent was slightly over $2,500 a month. I knew at this point it was best to postpone the housing search and start looking for a high-paying job. I had no plan, or even an idea, as to what I was doing. I just knew that I wanted to live in Los Angeles and that I was going to make it happen.

After many Google searches, I was exhausted and decided I was done for the day, but then something magical happened. Right before I closed my laptop for the night, I saw an impeccable landscape photograph that depicted Los Angeles. I liked the picture, so I saved it as my desktop wallpaper and said aloud, "God, I know you are sending me to Los Angeles this summer, and for that, I am thanking you now."

Corbin was in the room silently working on homework at the time. When he heard me speak he looked up and said, "Did you say something? Who are you talking to?"

Embarrassed that he may have heard what I said, I replied, "No one."

I closed my laptop and went to sleep that night, knowing something good was going to happen.

After that night, I decided I wanted to go to Los Angeles and the race was on. I began emailing everyone I could at whatever companies I knew of inquiring about internships. Weeks passed by; finals were in session and students began to hear back from companies they applied to in March regarding their internships. Unfortunately, I had heard from no one at the time. Since I decided I wanted to go to Los Angeles so late, I had no real applications in, let alone an interview. My drive and passion began to fade away as I saw no progress in my journey. Discouraged, one day I went to the mall with some friends to have some fun. I wanted to distract myself from my LA hunt and decompress. Following a lot of window shopping and people watching, I went to a bar to look at a basketball game and grab some chicken wings. Anyone who knows me knows I love a good cocktail, buffalo wings, and blue cheese dressing. Yum!

As I was walking into the bar my professor, Prof. Adisa Iwa was walking out of the bar.

"Mr. Sumlin! How are you, sir?" he yelled over the loudness of the bar crowd.

"I'm well," I replied.

I thought our conversation was going to be brief and cordial, but it was more than expected. Prof. Iwa pulled me to the side and asked me a question.

"Do you know of any students who will be in LA this summer? A friend of mine reached out to me from a major entertainment firm asking for a Morehouse student to come intern at her office."

Instantly after he said LA, I was floored. I felt like God had finally given me the break I yearned for so badly.

"I'll do it!" I replied with excitement. "I've been praying for an opportunity to intern in LA. If possible, I'd like to apply for the position."

At that moment, I didn't have any money, any housing or a plan, I just knew that I had the desire to go to LA that summer. I felt like a crazy man volunteering myself to apply like that. Of course, this was risky, but like Tyra Banks says, "Big risk, big reward." So I just went for it.

"Great!" Prof. Iwa said. "Please send me an email reminding me to follow up with my friends in LA, and we will be in touch. Have a good night."

As soon as my professor walked out of my sight, I pulled out my cell phone and sent him an email with my resume, reminding him of our conversation. After we had talked I was so pumped I ended up not even ordering food from that bar. I sent an email to Prof. Iwa, watched a couple of minutes of the game and left. My friends and I caught a taxi back to campus. The mall is about twenty minutes from campus, and I noticed that every traffic light we rode past in the taxi was green. Call me crazy, but I took this as a sign. For some reason, I just believed in my heart that this was God giving me the green light to go and chase my dream.

In a matter of days, the company that Prof. Iwa told me about reached out for an interview. They said it would be over the phone; I was so confident. I knew that this was for me and that I was going to get the job. The interview went well. I had peace knowing I did my best, and the company liked me. Following my interview, I got an email asking if I could fly out to Los Angeles to interview in person. I knew this wasn't an option for me because I knew no one out there and simply didn't have the means. Weeks went by; school was over, and I was away from Morehouse still not knowing a final decision.

After endless emails, I was finally notified that I did not get the job. I was told the other candidate was based in LA, and they were able to meet him personally. I was devastated. At the time I was in Gallatin, Tennessee, visiting my friend Russell when I saw the email. Russell's mom was cooking dinner, and I remember asking her if I could go for a walk in the neighborhood. I told her it was because it was such a lovely day and I wanted to experience the good weather. Truthfully, I wanted to go for a walk so I could cry and pray because I was deeply disappointed.

So there I was, walking down the streets of Gallatin, Tennessee, talking out loud and ugly crying. I began to ask God why. Why tease me with this opportunity? Why let all the lights be green on the way home? Was this all one big joke? Once I said all those words out loud, I asked God for a release. I told him I didn't want to be upset and that I trusted him. I began to have a paradigm shift and my words of prayer changed.

"Thank you, God, for the closed door. Thank you that this is going to make a great story for someone someday." Once I began to feel grateful, my sadness subsided. I knew that even though I did not get this opportunity that others would come. It was not the end of the world, and something good was meant to come out of this story.

The next day I returned home from Gallatin, Tennessee to Columbus, Ohio. I told my grandmother about my experience interviewing with this company and how long they had given me the runaround. She assured me that something good would come out of this situation.

Again, with a mind full of thoughts I went for a walk. The evening sky was beautiful. I was walking, yet I was still. Still in my mind and spirit;

I had a good feeling inside. It's something still I can't describe. It had to be God reassuring me that things were going to be okay.

After my walk, I went back home and got a phone call. It was the company I wanted to work for in LA. They told me the candidate they had wanted to accept the position had a family emergency and wasn't able to do the internship that summer.

When I heard this I figured they were calling me to ask if I would accept the offer, and luckily, I was right. They asked me if I was still interested in doing the internship. By that time it was late May, I was in Ohio and had no other plans.

I thought to myself, "Hell yeah I want to do the internship." I could not say that on the phone, or I might've lost the job again. So instead, I humbly replied, "Thank you so much for the offer. I gladly accept. When do I need to be in the office?"

"Monday," the HR specialist replied.

"Okay, I'll be there."

At this time, so much time had gone by, but I did not have any money. This was another example of me having faith and believing it would work out.

From there I coordinated with a Human Resources specialist, did some paperwork online, and the next day I was officially the 2015 summer intern for a major entertainment company in LA.

This was a big goal, it took a long time, but I finally had a job offer in Los Angeles. The next part was trying to find housing and buy a flight.

My mom was so excited that I had a job in Los Angeles, but she was really concerned about where I would live and how I would get there. To be honest, I was really concerned too, but I had to keep the faith. I kept believing something would eventually work out.

Once I got the job, I called Prof. Iwa. I figured if he had friends in Los Angeles maybe he could find me a place to stay. Before I knew it, he sent out a mass email to all his Morehouse friends in Los Angeles and the Morehouse College Parent Association. After he had done that I began to receive random phone calls from all kinds of people. The Morehouse community in Los Angeles is very strong, and they all stay in touch with one another.

Word got around quickly about my new internship and my need for housing. It was a Wednesday when I officially got the job, and I knew I had to be on the job by that Monday. During those few days, I remember being really overwhelmed by all that was going on. Because of all that was going on, I didn't have time to really grasp and digest it all. The only thing on my mind was how I could execute this plan, and what did I need to do to actually work the job.

The days following my job acceptance were hectic. I was getting phone calls at all hours of the night from people in Los Angeles who had housing offers for me. I had never been out to the West Coast before, so I never took into account the three-hour time difference from Cali to Ohio. For me, it was 10:00 p.m. and 7:00 p.m. there. The late night phone calls took some getting used to, but it worked out.

By the weekend, my mother and grandmother had gotten all the money I needed for my flight to Los Angeles. I do not know how they found the money at such short notice, but they did, and the flight was soon booked, and I was good to go. Things began to calm down a little bit. I had a job, I had a flight, and now all I needed was a place to stay.

My flight was on Monday, and that Sunday night I received a call from a random phone number with an area code based out of Los Angeles. I knew I could not be selective and not answer the phone even though it was late, so I answered.

"Hello?"

"Hi, is this Chris Sumlin?"

"Yes, this is, how's it going?" I said in my most enthusiastic voice.

"Hi, I'm well. I'm Bobbette Glover, and my husband and I heard your story, and we want to help."

Again, God was looking out for me. I had no idea who this woman was, and she had no idea who I was, but she wanted to help.

"Our son Jamal graduated from Morehouse in 2013, and we have an extra bedroom. You are more than welcome to stay with us temporarily until we can find you a more permanent place."

I was taken back by her generosity, and I gladly accepted her offer.

"Text me tomorrow morning what you are wearing and my husband, Larry, and I will get you from the airport and show you around."

It was a long journey that took a couple of months, but that next morning I said my goodbyes to my family and flew out to Los Angeles to intern at 20th Century FOX. It was such a long road that required a lot of faith, but when my feet finally landed in Los Angeles on that bright and sunny day all I could say was, "Thank you, God, for helping me hold on."

Life doesn't always go our way or according to our plan. My grandmother always tells me, "Life is what happens when you're busy making plans." Those words are so true. Often, we want things so badly our way, on our time, but God will have a different plan. The key is to hold on and remember why you started. I promise you, your life is perfect! You are a superstar. You were built to live the life presented to you. Every heartache, every closed door and missed opportunity that you encounter is part of a master plan. Next time you face hardship, be grateful! Say out loud:

"Thank you for this closed door."

"Thank you that this is working for my good."

With that perspective, you will always come out okay. The really big moments in life come with the greatest turmoil and turbulence. Going after a big dream you will have opposition, but it is important to keep holding on. I can't discuss or write about anything that I have not lived, but if there is something that I know for sure it is that if you hold on even when it's tough, things will go your way. Just believe in yourself, keep the faith and hold on.

Thank you, Nanny, for that phone conversation we had when I thought all hope was lost. You taught me a valuable lesson to always hold on. You always believe in me even when I forget to believe in myself. Thank you, Prof. Iwa, for believing in me when I wasn't even sure that I could do this. And thank you, Bobbette and your husband Larry, who welcomed me into your home with nothing but love and generosity. Thank you.

I AM SEED:

I am so happy my life is perfectly unfolding for my highest and best.

12

KEEP THE VISION

WHEN I LANDED AT THE LA AIRPORT to start my internship I was so excited. A mother and father of a Morehouse grad came and picked me up from the airport and took me to lunch. When I walked out those airport doors, I was in awe of the bright West Coast sun and the beautiful palm trees. I thought to myself, here I am in a new city with all these new things to explore. I was so grateful and honored just to be there. As my host parents and I rode around the city, I was fascinated by the abundance of wealth and fancy cars LA had to offer. Everywhere I turned and walked I saw Rolls Royces, Bentleys, and even Lamborghinis. When I saw those cars, I felt rich. I felt that it wasn't a big deal that I saw cars like this at every red light. I knew I was adapting to the city fairly quickly.

Riding through the city, I saw signs that read "Hollywood" and "Beverly Hills." I felt like I was on a reality TV show. My host mother was giving me a tour of the city and informed me of all the great people who lived around. She told me how she had experienced great concerts and seen a lot of famous people.

She looked at me and said, "Chris, have you met anyone famous during your time at Morehouse?"

"Yes," I humbly replied. " I have met Rihanna, Tyler Perry, and a whole lot of others I can't name. I'm over the celebrity meeting, though. The only celebrity I would really love to meet now is Kim Kardashian."

My host mother informed me how Kim Kardashian lived in Calabasas and traveled through LA often. My heart got excited because I knew that if I could meet all those other stars I had met thus far that I could meet Kim Kardashian-West.

We drove around for hours and hours. It was fun. Los Angeles seemed very spread out to me and traffic was insane. When we finally arrived at the house in which I would be staying, I jumped right into bed without even unpacking. I'll never forget my first night in Los Angeles. I was thinking of how badly I wanted to be in LA and work there. I was deeply anxious about meeting more stars and celebrities. That night I remember going through my phone and seeing an old picture I created. The picture I pulled up was a photoshopped image of myself and Kim Kardashian. I made the picture earlier that year out of faith that I would one day meet her. That night I made the picture the lock screen on my phone.

I am a deep believer in the Law of Attraction. I have always believed that whatever images you feed yourself and your mind you can attract into your life. This is one of my secrets to success. When dealing with life, our goals can sometimes be so unrealistic and unfathomable. I know the benefits of dreaming big; it's an awesome thing to do but sometimes it's discouraging. One thing I do with all my goals is visualize them first, and then watch them manifest. This is the same concept a lot of self-help teachers discuss when teaching the idea of vision boards.

If you're not into self-help books, this all may sound kind of odd or you may feel out of your element. Let me conceptualize this big idea for you with an example.

Imagine you want to buy a pair of shoes. You know the brand, the model, the color, and everything. You know that these shoes are expensive and to get them it will be a challenge. This is a perfect situation for you to try the "Keep the Vision" lesson in your life. Here's what I suggest you do:

Get informed. Learn all you can about the shoes. Become obsessed! Eat, live and breathe the shoes.

Visualize it. Get pictures of the shoes off the Internet, magazines or books, and keep those pictures around you wherever you go. They can be on your phone or hung up in your room. Either way, the pictures need to be seen by you every day. (This is the visualization part.)

Say it like you mean it. Tell everyone you can how you are buying the shoes, and deeply believe your words when telling people about what it is you're doing. (This will take practice, but I promise it works.)

Watch for the signs. Keep your eyes open for any way to make your goal of receiving the shoes happen, and watch it manifest! I know for sure that when you set a goal seriously, life will send you signs to make it happen. Always look out for those signs.

That was very fast, but follow my Kim Kardashian manifestation story, and it will make more sense.

My first night in Los Angeles was the day I started my "keep the vision" concept with the idea of meeting Kim Kardashian. I had my "Chris Sumlin, Kim Kardashian" lock screen, some faith, and I was in LA. I knew that there was no way I would leave the city without meeting that woman somehow, some way.

The next day, following my flight to Los Angeles, I started working at my internship at 20th Century FOX. I met lots of great people. At my job I was informed that stars were frequent at work. Many of them would come to pitch shows and have meetings. When I made my runs around the office meeting, everyone kept advising me to play it cool if I saw someone famous on the lot. I had already known this concept of visualization, so I figured this was my opportunity to apply "say it like I mean it." When someone told me about meeting famous people on the lot I always responded and said, "I've met enough stars. The only star I am going to go crazy for WHEN (not if) I meet her is Kim Kardashian-West."

I told this to one of my coworkers, and she laughed and said, "Why would you want to meet Kim Kardashian? She's a reality star and super famous. You'll probably never meet someone of her caliber anyway."

For some reason that didn't resonate with me at all; I just knew she was wrong. I believed I was going to meet Kim Kardashian no matter what. Weeks went by, and nothing happened. I kept believing it would happen someday. I had Kim's tweets sent to my phone, and I told myself every day that I was going to meet her. At this moment, I still had the photoshopped picture of her and me on my phone. I genuinely believed that it would happen. My internship at FOX was only for ten weeks. Nine of those weeks went by, and then something amazing happened.

I remember that Monday. I was on the bus commuting to work, and I saw a tweet from Kim Kardashian. The tweet was one inviting all of Kim Kardashian's fans to her boutique for a meet and greet and picture. This was it. This was the moment I was waiting on. I was so excited; I felt with every fiber in my being that this was my shot. That day of work is one I remember very vividly. I couldn't even lie to my boss that Monday morning when I went to her and told her I would be late for work on Thursday. My supervisor at the time was a woman named Kaliko Hurley. She's one of the coolest bosses I've ever had. That morning when she walked in, I saw her and knew we had to have a conversation. I went over to her desk that morning and modestly said, "Kaliko, we need to talk."

"What's wrong?" she replied.

"Umm… I won't be at work until later on Thursday because something has come up."

At this moment I started to go on and tell some sob story and make something up, but honesty is truly the best policy.

I picked my head up and said, "Kim Kardashian is having a meet and greet on Thursday, and I really want to go. Is it okay if I come in a little late on Thursday?"

She was silent for a minute, and I thought to myself, "You blew it, you're gonna get fired. Just start apologizing and crying." Nonetheless, Kaliko didn't fire me. She told me to have a good time and make sure I was caught up on all my work. When she said that, I felt so relieved. I knew there was nothing that could hold me back from meeting Kim Kardashian. The rest of the week flew by, and before I could call it, it was Thursday—the day of the big event.

The day of the meet and greet I woke up at 5:00 a.m., pumped that I was going to meet Kim K. The boutique was relatively close to my apartment so I thought it would be a good idea to walk all the way to the location. It was a beautiful sunny LA day. The wind was just right; the sun was shining brightly. Everything felt so good.

As I walked to the store, the entire time I walked I had a smile from ear to ear. I'm sure people looking at me were wondering why I was smiling so hard, but I couldn't hold in the excitement.

After walking two miles, I finally made it to the boutique. To my surprise, there were no more than fifteen people in line to meet Kim. The meet and greet started at noon, but I got there at 8:00 a.m. The wait was enjoyable, and everyone around was excited. Of course, I was the only black guy there. Around me were tons of young girls with their Kim Kardashian magazines and apparel. The energy was crazy. Once I heard how much everyone loved Kim it made me even more ready to meet her. Girls were sharing their favorite pictures and videos of Kim online. It was truly a magical moment that a lot of us in line were really looking forward to.

Time went by. It was 11:30 a.m. and the line stepped to the front door. My heart began to race, and I started sweating. All I could think of was the picture I had photoshopped, all the believing, and the doubters who told me it would never happen. I thought I was going to faint. More time went by, and before I knew it, I was in the boutique. The workers there were so friendly. They informed me we had to buy the book to meet her. That had to be the happiest I've ever been to buy a book.

"Here's my cash!" I stated to a sales associate.

"Awesome, you're all set. Make sure you smile," she responded.

I had the book in-hand and was moving up the line. I turned to my right, and there she was: Kim Kardashian-West!

She looked so beautiful, and as soon as I saw her I started cheering. Everyone began to look at me as if I had lost my mind. I stood there next in line, and there were some fans from London meeting the reality star. I couldn't get over the fact that Kim was there in all her prettiness and fame. She was so nice to those London fans. It was a mother and two children. She thanked the mother so much for bringing her kids there, as if she truly benefitted from their presence. Kim's voice was so soft but it wasn't fresh; it seemed that she may have been under the weather that day. I was amazed at her apparent humility and heart. After the family from London got their picture I was up next.

So many thoughts ran through my mind. What am I going to say? Will she even remember me? I wondered how she felt because she was pregnant and all. All of these thoughts and questions subsided when the boutique employee said, "Next!" I knew this was my moment. I went to Kim Kardashian and full of energy I said, "Hi, I am Chris Sumlin. I am such a huge fan of yours. I love everything about you."

She just looked at me, smiled and said, "Thank you." We took our picture. After the picture was over, I looked back at Kim and her head was down.

"Did you pick your head up in the pic, sis? I hope you smiled!" I said to Kim.

"I did, I promise," she said while smiling. It was so crazy! After I took the picture all the security guards were clapping and looking at me like I had won an award. It was a dream come true.

That was another goal accomplished. I went to work directly after that and told everyone of my adventure. It was interesting because those same ones who said it would never happen, were the same ones who acknowledged how cool of an experience meeting Kim had to have been.

The lesson to learn from this entire story is to keep the vision in front of you. Some of you reading this may not like Kim Kardashian, or think standing in lines to meet someone is just flat out stupid, but the principle isn't. Whatever goal you have for yourself, go for it. Speak that thing daily. Every time I went to work for over eight weeks I said to myself, "I am going to meet Kim Kardashian." Who would have thought a pregnant Kim K. would host a meet and greet in my neighborhood just a week before my internship ended? I believe that this happened simply because I set the vision, believed it and allowed it to happen. I challenge you to do the same thing. If you want a house, go online and pick one, forget about your credit or your money, just pick one. Print it out, frame the picture and put it next to your bed, and each morning say to yourself, "I am moving into that new home." Maybe you want to attend a college. Go online, order a T-shirt from that college's bookstore and wear it as often as you can. Speak to yourself each time you wear it, "This is the college I am going to."

Many people have the perspective that life happens to you. I believe that life happens with you. I know for sure that every moment we experience is a product of our thoughts. I just really believe that. I believe that God and I work simultaneously to co-create my reality. You have the same capacity to do what I did. I am in no way different from you. So step up and get to work.

Anything you want in life is possible to obtain, but you have to believe that it is. You can apply this principle to every aspect of your life. Now that you have learned this I am excited to see the things you visualize for yourself.

Thank you, Kim Kardashian! You have no idea what your meet and greet taught me about visualization. You were so kind to me, and our picture on Facebook was my most liked post ever. I hope you read this book and are happy to know that you inspired me and taught me a big lesson.

I AM SEED:

I am keeping visions of my goals because they are going to happen!

ABOUT THE AUTHOR
CHRIS SUMLIN

CHRISTOPHER MICHAEL SUMLIN was born in Dayton, Ohio, destined for Greatness. He comes from a tight-knit family, with two brothers and a younger sister. He grew up in a Christian household. His father was a minister and church was the basis of Chris's young adult life.

At age 14, Chris attended a high school called The Charles School at Ohio Dominican University in Columbus, Ohio. With the love and support of family and mentors, Chris graduated from the school in five years earning both his high school diploma and Associate of Arts degree from Ohio Dominican University.

Chris currently attends the historic Morehouse College in Atlanta, Georgia majoring in Cinema, Television & Emerging Media Studies. In the summer of 2015, Chris interned at both FOX Studios and the BET Awards in Los Angeles, California.

You can find out more about Chris at **www.thechrissumlin.com.**